crocheted throws & wraps

crocheted throws & wraps

25 throws, wraps and blankets to crochet

MELODY GRIFFITHS

CICO BOOKS
LONDON NEW YORK

This edition published in 2017 by CICO Books

An imprint of Ryland Peters & Small Ltd
20–21 Jockey's Fields, London, WC1R 4BW
341 E 116th St, New York, NY 10029

www.rylandpeters.com

10 9 8 7 6 5 4 3 2 1

First published in 2009 by CICO Books

A CIP catalogue record for this book is available from the British Library.

ISBN: 978 1 78249 486 7

Printed in China

Editor: Marie Clayton
Designer: David Fordham
Photography: Carolyn Barber except pages 15, 19, 20, 21, 40, 41, 65, 66, 67 and 120 by Beckie Maynes
Pattern checker: Susan Horan
Illustrators: Michael Hill and Stephen Dew

contents

introduction

To me, one of the most fascinating things about crochet is that it can be incredibly inventive and flexible, but at the same time it can also be simple and comfortingly repetitive. In this collection I have tried to combine these two elements to achieve original, unusual designs that are easy to work. Afghans, comforters, coverlets or throws – whatever you call them – are such satisfying things to create and make wonderful gifts for every age and occasion. I hope that you'll find something here that's right for you and your lifestyle in each of the four chapters in this book.

The Vintage Style section is in the soft, creamy colours of antique fabrics. Two of the designs echo heirloom crochet lace, while traditional knits are the starting place for a beautiful crochet version of a Shetland lace shawl and an Argyll diamonds design in fast working treble groups. Fabrics from the thirties and fifties inspired the charming puffs baby blanket, the richly textured pale green blanket and the classic gingham blanket.

The American Dream section includes designs based on a wide range of pieced quilts and homespun weaving. The pared down style of the Shaker sect is shown in a simple throw, while the contrasting colours found in Amish quilts inspired the sunshine and shadow throw. I have tried to echo the way that a simple motif can be arranged to make a larger design in my interpretation of a Navajo blanket, and a motif based on intricate Seminole patchwork was scaled up to make a blanket that's just like an abstract painting. Pioneer patchwork quilts gave me the idea for the log cabin coverlet and the crazy patchwork throw.

For my next theme I wanted to bring the Outside Inside so the designs are inspired by the natural world. If you like making pictures, there's a rainbow striped blanket in vibrant colours, a landscape play blanket that's like a child's drawing and a seascape wall hanging that started out as a watercolour sketch. There are three designs based on flowers: a perfect, classic throw that uses a myriad of colours to work alternating squares in rose and daisy motifs; a flower garden throw with daisy motifs; and a wild flower throw where simple triangles make four-petal flowers set in openwork squares.

The designs in the Around the World section are inspired by a range of textiles and techniques. The patterns found on Aran sweaters were interpreted in raised crochet stitches to make a richly textured throw. Scottish plaid rugs inspired the tartan blanket, and knitwear motifs were worked in cross stitch on a crochet background to make the Scandinavian sampler throw. Eastern Mediterranean carpet designs gave me a starting point for the kelim runner, a beaded table mat from Africa triggered off the circular throw and Japanese woven textiles gave me the feel for the ikat throw.

For me, this has been an incredibly satisfying book to work on. It has been inspiring to look at fabrics, hand-made crafts, textiles and motifs from all around the world, then to interpret them in crochet. I hope that you are inspired to be creative too.

chapter 1 *vintage style*

cream
comforter

Here's all the excitement of a traditional whitework bedcover, but made from easy-to-work, pared down blocks finished with a pretty picot edging and joined with a decorative trim to give an old-fashioned effect in less time.

SIZE
133 x 98cm (52¼ x 38½in)

YOU WILL NEED
11 x 50g balls of Debbie Bliss Rialto DK in cream
4.00mm (US F/5) crochet hook

TENSION
Each square measures 20 x 20cm (8 x 8in) measured across straight edges, 28 x 28cm (11 x 11in) measured from point to point, using 4.00mm (US F/5) hook. Change hook size, if necessary, to obtain this size square.

ABBREVIATIONS
beg = beginning; **ch** = chain; **dc** = double crochet; **foll** = following; **rem** = remaining; **rep** = repeat; **RS** = right side; **sp** = space; **ss** = slip stitch; **st(s)** = stitch(es); **tr** = treble; **2trtog** = leaving last loop of each tr on hook, work 2tr, yrh and pull through 3 loops on hook; **3trtog** = leaving last loop of each tr on hook, work 3tr, yrh and pull through 4 loops on hook; **yrh** = yarn around hook; **[ ]** = work instructions in square brackets as directed.

lacy square

Make 10ch, ss in first ch to form a ring.

1st round (RS): 1ch, 1dc in ring, 2ch, 23tr in ring, ss in 2nd ch.

2nd round: 1ch, 1dc in same place as ss, 5ch, [miss 1tr, 1tr in next tr, 3ch] 11 times, ss in 2nd ch.

3rd round: 1ch, 1dc in same place as ss, 2ch, * 2ch, 1dc in next 3ch sp, 2ch, [1tr in next tr, 3tr in next 3ch sp] twice, 1tr in foll tr, rep from * 3 more times omitting last tr, ss in 2nd ch.

4th round: [Ss, 1ch, 1dc] in first 2ch sp, [8ch, 1dc in next 2ch sp, 2ch, miss 1tr, 1tr in each of next 7tr, 2ch, miss 1tr, 1dc in next 2ch sp] 4 times omitting last dc, ss in first dc.

5th round: Ss in first 8ch sp, 1ch, 1dc in 8ch sp, 2ch, 10tr in same 8ch sp, [2ch, miss 1tr, 1tr in each of next 5tr, 2ch, miss 1tr, 11tr in next 8ch sp] 3 times, 2ch, miss 1tr, 1tr in each of next 5tr, 2ch, miss 1tr, ss in 2nd ch.

6th round: 1ch, 1dc in same place as ss, 3ch, [1tr in next tr, 1ch] 9 times, 1tr in foll tr, * 2ch, miss 1tr, 1tr in each of next 3tr, 2ch, miss 1tr, [1tr in next tr, 1ch] 10 times, 1tr in foll tr, rep from * two more times, 2ch, miss 1tr, 1tr in each of next 3tr, 2ch, miss 1tr, ss in 2nd ch.

7th round: 1ch, 1dc in same place as ss, 4ch, [1tr in next tr, 2ch] 4 times, * [1tr, 4ch, 1tr] in foll tr, 2ch, [1tr in next tr, 2ch] 5 times, miss 1tr, 1tr in foll tr, 2ch, miss 1tr, [1tr in next tr, 2ch] 5 times, rep from * two more times, [1tr, 4ch, 1tr] in foll tr, 2ch, [1tr in next tr, 2ch] 5 times, miss 1tr, 1tr in foll tr, 2ch, miss 1tr, ss in 2nd ch.

8th round: [Ss, 1ch, 1dc] in first 2ch sp, 2ch, [5ch, 1dc in 5th ch from hook, 1tr in next 2ch sp] 4 times, * 5ch, 1dc in 5th ch from hook, [1tr, 5ch, 1dc in 5th ch from hook,] twice in next 4ch sp, 1tr in same 4ch sp **, [5ch, 1dc in 5th ch from hook, 1tr in next 2ch sp] 12 times, rep from * two more times, then rep from * to **, [5ch, 1dc in 5th ch from hook, 1tr in next 2ch sp] 7 times, 5ch, 1dc in 5th ch from hook, ss in 2nd ch.
Fasten off.

comforter

Make 18 lacy squares. Darn in ends and press. Lay squares out with RS facing in alternate lines of four squares and three squares turned on their points, so giving five lines of squares.

to make up

Join 1st line of squares

With RS facing, join yarn in first 5ch picot along one edge of first square, 2ch, 2trtog in same picot as join, working down first edge of first square [3ch, 3trtog in next picot] 14 times, 6ch, 3trtog in first picot of one edge of 2nd square, complete first edge in same way as first square, ending 6ch, then work down adjacent edge in the same way, 6ch, work along two edges of 3rd square and up one edge of 4th square in the same way, ending 6ch.

Join 2nd line of squares

3trtog in first picot of 5th square, [1ch, ss in next 3ch sp of 4th square, 1ch, 3trtog in next picot of 5th square] 14 times, 3ch, ss in 6ch sp between 4th and 3rd squares, 3ch, join adjacent edge of 5th square to 3rd square, then join 6th square to 3rd and 2nd squares and 7th square to 2nd and first squares in the same way, ending 6ch.

Join 3rd line of squares

Work edging on rem 2 sides of 7th, 6th and 5th squares, ending 3ch, ss in 6ch sp, 3ch. Working in the same way, join one edge of 8th square and one edge of 9th square to 5th square, adjacent edge of 9th square and one edge of 10th square to 6th square, then adjacent edge of 10th square and one edge of 11th square to 7th square, ending 3ch, ss in 6ch sp, 3ch, ss in top of 2trtog at beg of first square.

Fasten off.

Join 4th line of squares

Rejoin yarn to opposite corner of 11th square. Work edging on one side of 11th square, rem 2 sides of 10th and 9th squares and one side of 8th square, ending 6ch. Working in the same way, join one edge of 12th square to 8th square, adjacent edge of 12th square and one edge of 13th square to 9th square, adjacent edge of 13th square and one edge of 14th square to 10th square and adjacent edge of 14th square to 11th square, ending 6ch.

Join 5th line of squares

Work edging on rem 2 sides of 14th, 13th and 12th squares, ending 3ch, ss in 6ch sp, 3ch. Working in the same way, join one edge of 15th square and one edge of 16th square to 12th square, join adjacent edge of 16th square and one edge of 17th square to 13th square, then join adjacent edge of 17th square and one edge of 18th square to 14th square, ending 3ch, ss in 6ch sp, 3ch, ss in 2trtog at beg of 11th square.

Darn in ends. Press lightly on WS.

charted version of 1st and 7th rounds of lacy square

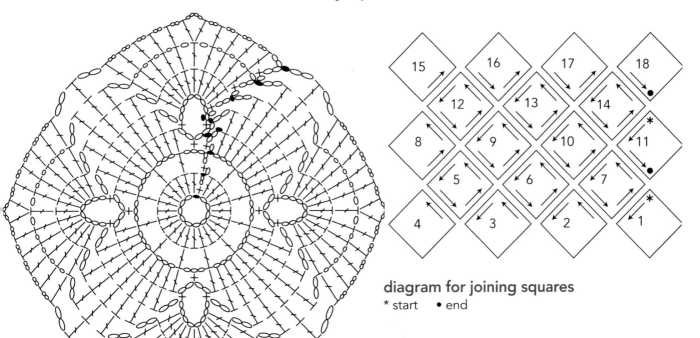

diagram for joining squares
* start   • end

15	16	17	18
12	13	14	* 11
8	9	10	
			*
4	5	3	6	7	1

key

○ **ch** = chain

● **ss** = slip stitch

+ **dc** = double crochet

T **tr** = treble

pale green
textured blanket

*Inspired by classic waffle stitch blankets, this crochet version
in soft, thick roving yarn is the ultimate in luxury.*

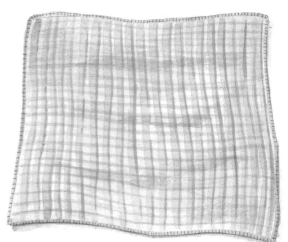

SIZE
85 x 109cm (33½ x 43in)

YOU WILL NEED
22 x 50g balls of Debbie Bliss Como in pale green
9.00mm (US M/13) crochet hook

TENSION
6 sts measure 8cm (3⅛in), 4 rows measure 7cm
(2¾in) over puff stitch and double crochet patt,
using 9.00mm (US M/13) hook. Change hook
size, if necessary, to obtain this tension.

ABBREVIATIONS
ch = chain; **cont** = continue; **dc** = double
crochet; **patt** = pattern; **rep** = repeat; **RS** =
right side; **ss** = slip stitch; **st(s)** = stitch(es); **yrh**
= yarn around hook; **[ ]** = work instructions in
square brackets as directed.

NOTES
• The usual starting chain edge can be too tight
so, to avoid this, working the first row over a
length of yarn is explained at the start of the
instructions. This gives a soft, flexible edge that
can be eased out to the full width of the fabric.
• Each loop of the puff stitch should be pulled
up to measure about 2.5cm (1in).

make a matching cushion
If you'd like to make a cushion cover to
match the blanket, you'll need 4 x 50g balls
of Como to make a 50 x 50cm (19½ x 19½in)
cushion front. Work in same way as blanket
making 37dc over yarn on first row and
continuing in pattern for 27 rows, or until
cushion front measures 50cm (19½in), before
edging with double crochet in the same way
as the blanket.

blanket
Leaving a 120cm (48in) length of yarn free, make slip knot on
hook.
1st row (RS): 1ch, work 61dc over free end of yarn. 61 sts.
2nd row: 1ch, 1dc in first dc, * lengthen loop on hook slightly,
[yrh, insert hook in side strand of previous dc, yrh and pull
through] 3 times, yrh and pull through 7 loops on hook, miss 1dc,
1dc in next dc, rep from * 29 more times.
3rd row: 1ch, [1dc in top two strands of each st] to end. 61 sts.
2nd and 3rd rows form puff st and dc patt.
Cont in patt, work 57 more rows, so ending with a 2nd patt row.
Do not fasten off. Ease lower edge to same width as top edge and
secure loose ends.

edging
With pins or tags of contrast thread, mark centre of each side
edge, then mark centre of each half to give four equal sections on
each side.
1st round (RS): 1ch, 2dc in first dc, 1dc in each of next 59 sts, 3dc
in corner dc, work 20dc in each of the four marked sections up
first side edge, 3dc in corner dc, working alternately into space
next to puff st and over strand of yarn and dc of 1st row, work 1dc
in each of next 59 sts, 3dc in corner dc, work 20dc in each of the
four marked sections along 2nd side edge, 1dc in same place as
first 2dc, ss in first dc, turn.
2nd round: 1ch, 2dc in same place as ss, * 1dc in each dc to
corner, 3dc in corner dc, rep from * 3 more times omitting last
2dc, ss in first dc.
Fasten off.

to make up
Darn in ends. Press lightly on WS.

circular
coverlet

Inspired by an antique doily but scaled up to a coverlet size, this circular throw is worked in the round and has rings of flowers alternating with fast-to-work open mesh rounds.

SIZE
130cm (51in) across

YOU WILL NEED
19 x 50g balls of Debbie Bliss Cashmerino Aran in pale grey
5.00mm (US H/8) crochet hook

TENSION
1st to 7th rounds measure 20cm (8in) across, using 5.00mm (US H/8) hook. Change hook size, if necessary, to obtain this tension.

ABBREVIATIONS
ch = chain; **dc** = double crochet; **htr** = half treble; **rep** = repeat; **RS** = right side; **sp(s)** = space(s); **ss** = slip stitch; **tr** = treble; **2trtog** = leaving last loop of each tr on hook, work 2tr, yrh and pull through 3 loops on hook; **3trtog** = leaving last loop of each tr on hook, work 3tr, yrh and pull through 4 loops on hook; **WS** = wrong side; **yrh** = yarn around hook; **[ ]** = work instructions in square brackets as directed.

coverlet

Centre flower and 1st patterned band

Make 8ch, ss in first ch to form a ring.

1st round: 3ch, 2trtog in ring, 3ch, [3trtog, 3ch] 7 times in ring, ss in 2trtog.

2nd round: Ss in first 3ch sp, 1ch, 1dc in same 3ch sp, 5ch, [1dc in next 3ch sp, 5ch] 7 times, ss in first dc.

3rd round: Ss in first 5ch sp, [3ch, 2trtog, 5ch, 3trtog] in first 5ch sp, [3trtog, 5ch, 3trtog in next 5ch sp] 7 times, ss in 2trtog.

4th round: Ss in first 5ch sp, 3ch, 6tr in same 5ch sp, [1ch, 7tr in next 5ch sp] 7 times, 1dc in 3rd ch.

5th round: Ss in sp under dc of previous round, 1ch, 1dc in same sp, [5ch, miss 3 sts, 1dc in next tr, 5ch, miss 3 sts, 1dc in next 1ch sp] 8 times, omitting last dc, ss in first dc.

6th round: Ss in first 5ch sp, [3ch, 2trtog, 5ch, 3trtog] in first 5ch sp, [3trtog, 5ch, 3trtog in next 5ch sp] 15 times, ss in 2trtog.

7th round: Ss in first 5ch sp, 3ch, 6tr in same 5ch sp, 1ch, [7tr in next 5ch sp, 1ch] 15 times, ss in 3rd ch.

8th round: Ss in last 1ch sp of previous round, 1ch, 1dc in same sp, [5ch, miss 3 sts, 1dc in next tr, 5ch, miss 3 sts, 1dc in next 1ch sp] 15 times, 5ch, miss 3 sts, 1dc in next tr, 2ch, miss 3 sts, 1tr in first dc.

9th and 10th rounds: 1ch, 1dc in first sp, [5ch, 1dc in next 5ch sp] 31 times, 2ch, 1tr in first dc.
Fasten off.

1st ring of flowers, 1st flower

Make 8ch, ss in first ch to form a ring.

1st round: 3ch, 2trtog in ring, [5ch, 3trtog] 5 times in ring, 2ch, with WS together 1dc in last sp of 10th round, 2ch, work 7th petal in ring, 2ch, 1dc in next 5ch sp of 10th round, work 8th petal in ring, 5ch, ss in 2trtog.
Fasten off.

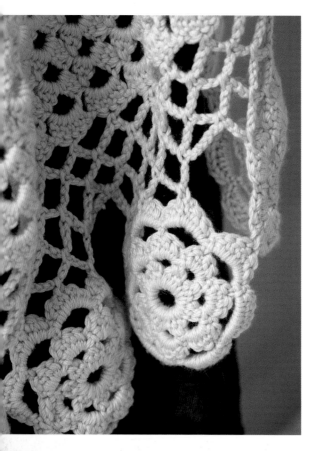

2nd flower

Work as given for first flower until 4 petals of first round have been completed, 2ch, with WS together 1dc in 2nd sp of 10th round on the left of first flower, 2ch, work 5th petal, 2ch, 1dc in next 5ch sp of 10th round, 2ch, work 6th petal, [2ch, 1dc in next free 5ch sp of previous flower, 2ch, work next petal in ring] twice, 5ch, ss in 2trtog. Fasten off.

Make and join 13 more flowers in same way as 2nd flower.

16th flower

Work as given for first flower until 2 petals have been completed, then make and join 2 petals to first flower, 2 petals to 10th round and 2 petals to 15th flower, 5ch, ss in 2trtog. Fasten off.

2nd patterned band

With RS facing, join yarn in a right-hand 5ch sp of a flower.

1st round: 1ch, 1dc in same sp as join, [5ch, 1dc in next 5ch sp of same flower, 5ch, 1dc over dc join between flowers, 5ch, 1dc in next 5ch sp of foll flower] 16 times omitting last 5ch and dc, 2ch, 1tr in first dc.

2nd and 3rd rounds: 1ch, 1dc in first sp, [5ch, 1dc in next 5ch sp] 47 times, 2ch, 1tr in first dc.

4th, 5th and 6th rounds: Ss in first 5ch sp, [3ch, 2trtog, 5ch, 3trtog] in first 5ch sp, [3trtog, 5ch, 3trtog in next 5ch] 47 times, ss in 2trtog.

7th round: Ss in first 5ch sp, 3ch, 6tr in same 5ch sp, [1ch, 7tr in next 5ch sp] 47 times, 1dc in 3rd ch.

8th round: Ss in sp under dc of previous round, 1ch, 1dc in same sp, [5ch, miss 3 sts, 1dc in next tr, 5ch, miss 3 sts, 1dc in next 1ch sp] 48 times, omitting last 5ch and dc, 2ch, 1tr in first dc.

9th, 10th and 11th rounds: 1ch, 1dc in first sp, [5ch, 1dc in next 5ch sp] 95 times, 2ch, 1tr in first dc. Fasten off.

2nd ring of flowers, 1st flower

1st round: Work as given for centre flower.

2nd round: Ss in first 3ch sp, [1dc, 1htr, 2tr, 1htr, 1dc] in each of first five 3ch sps, * [1dc, 1htr, 1tr] in next 3ch sp of flower, 1dc in 5ch sp of 11th round of 2nd patterned band, [1tr, 1htr, 1dc] in same 3ch sp of flower, rep from * two more times working into each of next two 5ch sps of 11th round, ss in first dc. Fasten off.

2nd flower

Work as first flower until 4 petals of 2nd round have been completed, make and join next petal to 3rd sp of 11th round to the left of previous flower, then make and join next 2 petals to next 2 sps of 11th round and last petal to adjacent sp of previous flower. Fasten off.

Make and join 29 more flowers the same way. Make and join 32nd flower to first flower, last 3 sps of 11th round and to 31st flower. Fasten off.

3rd patterned band
With RS facing, join yarn to first tr of centre petal of a flower.
1st round: 1ch, 1dc in same place as join, 5ch, 1dc in first tr of next petal of same flower, * [5ch, 1dc] in top of first tr of each of 3 petals of next flower, rep from * 30 more times, 5ch, 1dc in first tr of next petal of first flower, 2ch, 1tr in first dc.
2nd round: 1ch, 1dc in first sp, 5ch, 1dc in next 5ch sp, * [5ch, 1dc in 5ch sp between flowers] twice, [5ch, 1dc in next 5ch sp] twice, rep from * 30 more times, [5ch, 1dc in 5ch sp between flowers] twice, 2ch, 1tr in first dc.
3rd and 4th rounds: 1ch, 1dc in first sp, [5ch, 1dc in next 5ch sp] to last 5ch sp, 2ch, 1tr in first dc.
5th round: As 3rd and 4th rounds but ending 5ch, ss in first dc.
6th, 7th and 8th rounds: Ss in first 5ch sp, [3ch, 2trtog, 5ch, 3trtog] in first 5ch sp, [3trtog, 5ch, 3trtog in next 5ch sp] to end, ss in 2trtog.
9th round: Ss in first 5ch sp, 3ch, 4tr in same 5ch sp, 1ch, [5tr in next 5ch sp, 1ch] to end, ss in 3rd ch.
10th round: Ss in each of next 2tr, 1ch, 1dc in same place as last ss, [6ch, miss next 4tr, 1dc in foll tr] to end, miss last 4 sts, 3ch, 1tr in first dc.
11th, 12th and 13th rounds: 1ch, 1dc in first sp, [6ch, 1dc in next 6ch sp] to end, 3ch, 1tr in first dc.
Fasten off.

Last ring of flowers, 1st flower
1st round: Work as 1st round of centre flower.
2nd round: Ss in first 3ch sp, [1dc, 1htr, 2tr, 1htr, 1dc] in each 3ch sp, ss in first dc.
3rd round: Ss to first tr of first petal, 1ch, 1dc in same place as last ss, [5ch, 1dc in first tr of next petal] 7 times, 5ch, ss in first dc.
4th round: Ss in first 5ch sp, [1dc, 1htr, 4tr, 1htr, 1dc] in each of first 5 sps, * [1dc, 1htr, 2tr] in next 5ch sp of flower, 1dc in a 6ch sp of 13th round of 3rd pattern band, [2tr, 1htr, 1dc] in same 5ch sp of flower, rep from * two more times, joining into next 2 sps of 13th round, ss in first dc.
Fasten off.

2nd flower
Work as first flower until 4 petals of 4th round have been completed, make and join next petal to 4th 6ch sp of 13th round on left of first flower, then make and join next 2 petals to next two 6ch sps, leave one 6ch sp of 13th round free, make and join last petal to previous flower.
Fasten off.

Make and join 29 more flowers in same way as 2nd flower.
32nd flower
Work as first flower until 3 petals of 4th round have been completed, make and join next petal to first flower, leave next 6ch sp of 13th round free, make and join next 3 petals to next three 6ch sps of 13th round, leave next 6ch sp free, make and join last petal to previous flower.
Fasten off.

to make up
Darn in ends. Press lightly on WS.

make a cushion or a tablecloth
Cushion
You'll need just 2 x 50g balls of Cashmerino Aran to make a front for a round cushion 27cm (10½in) across. Simply work as given until the 10th round has been completed. If wished, add more rounds in dc or for a pretty finish work a shell edging in the same way as the edging on the Rainbow Baby Blanket on page 64.

Tablecloth
Simply work the design in fine cotton. Yarn amounts and hook sizes will vary depending on the weight of yarn chosen, so the best way to estimate is to start with just one ball and work the centre. If your tension is the same as given for the coverlet and you're happy with the result, check the amount of metres or yards to a ball of your chosen yarn. Calculate the number of balls you'll need to allow for approximately 1700 metres (1860 yards), adding extra in case you want to add more rounds of pattern and flowers.

shetland-style
shawl

This exquisite shawl was inspired by the undulating lacy stitch patterns seen on Shetland shawls. The centre is in a simple openwork chain stitch pattern worked in rows from corner to corner. The edging pattern is worked in rounds and finished with a pretty picot fan stitch border.

SIZE
95 x 95cm (37½ x 37½in)

YOU WILL NEED
7 x 50g balls of baby alpaca or pure wool DK in pale pink
6.00mm (US J/10) crochet hook

TENSION
Five 3ch sps and 6dc to 10cm (4in) over centre patt, one repeat worked on a base of 17dc along side edges measures 12cm (4¾in) and 5 rounds measure 10cm (4in) over old shale patt, shell edging measures 3.5cm (1⅜in), all using 6.00mm (US J/10) hook. Change hook size, if necessary, to obtain these tensions.

ABBREVIATIONS
ch = chain; **cont** = continue; **dc** = double crochet; **dtr** = double treble; **fan** = [1ch, 1dtr] 5 times, 1ch; **patt** = pattern; **rep** = repeat; **RS** = right side; **sp(s)** = space(s); **ss** = slip stitch; **st(s)** = stitch(es); **tr** = treble; **2trtog** = leaving last loop of each tr on hook work 1tr in each of next 2 sts, yarn around hook and pull through 3 loops on hook; **[ ]** = work instructions in square brackets as directed.

centre

Make 5ch, ss in first ch to form a ring.
1st row: 4ch, [3tr, 1ch, 1tr] in ring.
2nd row: 4ch, 3tr in 1ch sp, 3ch, [3tr, 1ch, 1tr] in 4ch sp.
3rd row: 4ch, 3tr in 1ch sp, 3ch, 1dc in 3ch sp, 3ch, [3tr, 1ch, 1tr] in 4ch sp. Two 3ch sps.
4th row: 4ch, 3tr in 1ch sp, [3ch, 1dc in next 3ch sp] twice, 3ch, [3tr, 1ch, 1tr] in 4ch sp. Three 3ch sps.
5th row: 4ch, 3tr in 1ch sp, [3ch, 1dc in next 3ch sp] 3 times, 3ch, [3tr, 1ch, 1tr] in 4ch sp. Four 3ch sps.
5th row forms chain mesh patt with 3tr at each end. Cont in patt working instructions in square brackets at centre one more time on each row until there are thirty-three 3ch sps and 34th row has been completed.
35th row: 3ch, miss 3tr, 3tr in first 3ch sp, [3ch, 1dc in next 3ch sp] 31 times, 3ch, 3tr in last 3ch sp, miss 3tr, 1tr in 4ch sp.
36th row: As 35th row, ending 1tr in end 3ch sp.
Working instructions in square brackets one less time on each row, cont in this way until there is one 3ch sp at centre.
Next row: 3ch, 3tr in 3ch sp, 1tr in end 3ch sp.
Next row: 3ch, 1dc in end sp, turn. Do not fasten off.

border

1st foundation round (RS): Ss in 3ch sp, 1ch, 2dc in same 3ch sp, [2dc in each row-end sp] to end of first 2 sides of square, 2dc in 5ch ring at corner, [2dc in each row-end sp] to end, ss in first dc. 272 sts.
From now on, work into back loop of sts on every round.

2nd foundation round: 4ch, 1dtr in same place as ss, 2dtr in each of next 2dc, miss 3dc, [1dc in each of foll 6dc, miss 3dc, 2dtr in each of next 2dc, 3dtr in foll dc, 2dtr in each of next 2dc, miss 3dc] 15 times, 1dc in each of next 6dc, miss 3dc, 2dtr in each of foll 2dc, 1dtr in same place as first dtr, ss in 4th ch. 272 sts.
Work in old shale patt.

1st round: 4ch, 1tr in same place as ss, 1ch, * [1tr, 1ch] in each of next 2dtr, ** [2trtog] 6 times, 1ch, [1tr, 1ch] in each of next 5dtr, rep from ** 2 more times, [2trtog] 6 times, 1ch, [1tr, 1ch] in each of next 2dtr, [1tr, 1ch] 3 times in foll dtr, rep from * 3 more times omitting last [1tr, 1ch] 3 times in foll dtr, 1tr in same place as first tr, 1ch, ss in 3rd ch. Count each ch as one st from now on. 288 sts.

2nd round: 4ch, 1tr in same place as ss, 1ch, * [1tr, 1ch] in each of next 4 sts, ** [2trtog] 6 times, 1ch, [1tr, 1ch] in each of next 5 sts, rep from ** 2 more times, [2trtog] 6 times, 1ch, [1tr, 1ch] in each of next 4 sts, [1tr, 1ch] 3 times in foll st, rep from * 3 more times omitting last [1tr, 1ch] 3 times in foll st, 1tr in same place as first tr, 1ch, ss in 3rd ch. 320 sts.

3rd round: 4ch, * [1tr, 1ch] in each of next 8 sts, ** [2trtog] 6 times, 1ch, [1tr, 1ch] in each of next 5 sts, rep from ** 2 more times, [2trtog] 6 times, 1ch, [1tr, 1ch] in each of next 9 sts, rep from * 3 more times omitting last [1tr, 1ch], ss in 3rd ch. 368 sts.

4th round: 4ch, * [miss 1ch, 1tr in next st, 1ch] 6 times, miss 1ch, 1tr in next st, ** [2trtog] 6 times, 1ch, [1tr, 1ch] in each of next 5 sts, rep from ** 2 more times, [2trtog] 6 times, 1tr in next st, [1ch, miss 1ch, 1tr in next st] 7 times, 1ch, rep from * 3 more times omitting last [1ch, miss 1ch, 1tr in next st], ss in 3rd ch. 344 sts.

5th round: 4ch, * [miss 1ch, 1tr in next st, 1ch] 5 times, miss 1ch, ** [2trtog] 6 times, 1ch, [1tr, 1ch] in each of next 5 sts, rep from ** 2 more times, [2trtog] 6 times, 1ch, [miss 1ch, 1tr in next st, 1ch] 6 times, rep from * 3 more times omitting last [miss 1ch, 1tr in next st, 1ch], ss in 3rd ch. 320 sts.

6th round: 4ch, * [1tr in next st, 1ch] 7 times, 1tr in next st, ** [2trtog] 6 times, 1ch, [1tr, 1ch] in each of next 5 sts, rep from ** 2 more times, [2trtog] 6 times, 1tr in next st, [1ch, 1tr in next st] 8 times, 1ch, rep from * 3 more times omitting last [1ch, 1tr in next st], ss in 3rd ch. 360 sts.

7th round: 4ch, * [miss 1ch, 1tr in next st, 1ch] 6 times, miss 1ch, ** [2trtog] 6 times, 1ch, [1tr, 1ch] in each of next 5 sts, rep from ** 2 more times, [2trtog] 6 times, 1ch, [miss 1ch, 1tr in next st, 1ch] 7 times, rep from * 3 more times omitting last [miss 1ch, 1tr in next st, 1ch], ss in 3rd ch. 336 sts.

8th round: 4ch, * [1tr in next st, 1ch] 9 times, 1tr in next st, ** [2trtog] 6 times, 1ch, [1tr, 1ch] in each of next 5 sts, rep from ** 2 more times, [2trtog] 6 times, 1tr in next st, [1ch, 1tr in next st] 10 times, 1ch, rep from * 3 more times omitting last [1ch, 1tr in next st], ss in 3rd ch. 392 sts.

9th round: 4ch, * [miss 1ch, 1tr in next st, 1ch] 8 times, miss 1ch, ** [2trtog] 6 times, 1ch, [1tr, 1ch] in each of next 5 sts, rep from ** 2 more times, [2trtog] 6 times, 1ch, [miss 1ch, 1tr in next st, 1ch] 9 times, rep from * 3 more times omitting last [miss 1ch, 1tr in next st, 1ch], ss in 3rd ch. 368 sts.

10th round: 1ch, 1dc in same place as ss, [1dc in each st] to end, ss in first dc.

shell border

Work into sts in the usual way from now on.

1st round (RS): 1ch, 1dc in same place as ss, * [miss 3dc, make fan in foll dc, miss 3dc, 1dc in next dc] 2 times, [miss 4dc, make fan in next dc, miss 3dc, 1dc in next dc, miss 3dc, make fan in foll dc, miss 3dc, 1dc in next dc] 4 times, miss 3dc, make fan in next dc, miss 3dc, 1dc in foll dc, rep from * 3 more times omitting last dc, ss in first dc.

2nd round: 5ch, [1dtr, 1ch] twice in same place as ss, [1dc in centre dtr of next fan, make fan in next dc] 43 times, 1dc in centre dtr of last fan, 1ch, [1dtr, 1ch] twice in same place as first 2dtr, ss in 4th ch.

Picot round: Ss in last 1ch sp of previous round, 1ch, 1dc in same place as ss, [3ch, ss in 3rd ch from hook, 1dc in next 1ch sp] twice, * 1dc in next sp, 1dc in next dc, 1dc in foll sp, [3ch, ss in 3rd ch from hook, 1dc in next 1ch sp] 4 times, rep from * 43 times, 1dc in next sp, 1dc in next dc, 1dc in foll sp, 3ch, ss in 3rd ch from hook, 1dc in next 1ch sp, 3ch, ss in 3rd ch from hook, ss in first dc. Fasten off.

to make up

Press on WS. Darn in ends.

puffs *baby blanket*

In the 1930s there was a craze for making a decorative patchwork from gathered circles of fabric, called Suffolk puffs or yo-yos. This pretty baby blanket echoes that style with ingeniously constructed, double thickness, two-round crochet puffs in pastel shades.

SIZE
54 x 63cm (21¼ x 24¾in)

YOU WILL NEED
Approximately:
35g of pure wool or wool rich 4ply yarn in pink
60g same in each of green and blue
45g same in each of mauve, lilac and yellow
50g same in turquoise
4.50mm (US G/6) and 2.50mm (US C/2) crochet hooks

TENSION
Each puff measures approximately 4.5cm (1¾in) across, using 4.50mm (US G/6) hook. Change hook size, if necessary, to obtain this size puff.

ABBREVIATIONS
ch = chain; **dc** = double crochet; **tr** = treble;
2trtog = leaving last loop of each tr on hook, work 1tr in each of next 2 sts, yrh and pull through 3 loops on hook; **trtr** = triple treble;
RS = right side; **ss** = slip stitch; **st(s)** = stitches;
WS = wrong side; **yrh** = yarn around hook;
[ ] = work instructions in square brackets as directed.

NOTES
• You can vary the amount of puffs you make in each colour as you wish or invent your own colour scheme but for the effect in the picture you'll need to make 17 puffs in pink, 31 in green, 30 in blue, 22 in mauve, 22 in lilac, 25 in turquoise and 21 in yellow.
• The puffs are worked using a larger hook than usual for 4ply yarn so that the double thickness motifs are lightweight.
• The decreases on the second round fold naturally to the wrong side.

for a larger blanket
Simply make more puffs and assemble them to the size you want. To help estimate the amount of yarn you'll need, allow approximately 20g for each extra 10 puffs.

puff
Using 4.50mm (US G/6) hook, make 5ch, ss in first ch to form a ring.
1st round (RS): 5ch, working over yarn end, make 19trtr in ring, ss in 5th ch. 20 sts.
2nd round: 2ch, leaving last loop on hook work 1tr in next trtr, yrh and pull through 2 loops on hook, [2trtog] 9 times, ss in 2nd ch. Leaving a long end, fasten off.
Make 168 puffs.

to make up
Darn in and trim starting end. Using long end, catch chain edge of 2nd round to WS of first round a little way from the centre opening.
Arrange puffs in a rectangle, 12 motifs across and 14 motifs down, on a piece of fabric. When you are happy with the arrangement, pin puffs in place. If you prefer, you could simply join puffs at random.
1st line of puffs: Using 2.50mm (US C/2) hook and with WS facing, join appropriate colour yarn in a trtr of first puff. With RS together, hold 2nd puff behind.
Joining row: Inserting hook in same trtr as join and in corresponding trtr of 2nd puff together, work 1dc, [1ch, 1dc in next trtr of each motif together] twice. Fasten off.
Leaving 7trtr at each side free, join 3trtr of 2nd puff to 3rd puff. Continue joining puffs in this way until 12 puffs have been joined.
2nd line of puffs: Count 5trtr back from join in 1st puff and join first 3 of these 5trtr to13th puff in the same way. Leaving 2trtr between joins each time, join 14th puff to 13th and 2nd puffs. Continue joining puffs in this way until 14 lines of puffs have been completed.
Darn in ends. If necessary, press very lightly on WS.

argyll *afghan*

The design for this afghan is taken from the classic diamond pattern found on socks and jumpers, scaled up and worked in a simple treble groups stitch pattern to make a lightweight comforter.

SIZE
74 x 104cm (29 x 41in)

YOU WILL NEED
3 x 50g balls of Sirdar Balmoral in each of pale grey (A) and pink (B)
2 x 50g balls same in pale blue (C)
1 x 50g ball same in cream (D)
4.00mm (US F/5) crochet hook

TENSION
Three 3tr and 3ch sp groups measure 9cm (3½in), 7 rows to 10cm (4in) over patt, using 4.00mm (US F/5) hook. Change hook size, if necessary, to obtain this tension.

ABBREVIATIONS
ch = chain; cont = continue; dc = double crochet; patt = pattern; rep = repeat; RS = right side; sp = space; ss = slip stitch; st(s) = stitch(es); tr = treble; WS = wrong side; [ ] = work instructions in square brackets as directed.

NOTES
• The afghan is worked from side to side.
• When changing colours, pull through the last loop of the last stitch in the old colour with the new colour. When the new colour has to be carried over a space, leaving a loose strand, catch the new colour in when working the first part of the treble, work the chain over the strand and catch the strand in with the first treble in the new colour.

afghan
Using A, make 203ch.

1st row (WS): 1tr in 4th ch from hook, 1tr in next ch, [3ch, miss 3ch, 1tr in each of next 3ch] 33 times.

2nd row: Using A, 1dc in first tr, 2ch, 1tr in each of next 2tr, [3tr in next 3ch sp, 3ch] 4 times, * using B, 3tr in foll 3ch sp, using A, [3ch, 3tr in next 3ch sp] 7 times, 3ch, rep from * two more times, using B, 3tr in foll 3ch sp, using A, [3ch, 3tr in next 3ch sp] 4 times, 1tr in each of last 3 sts.

3rd row: Using A, 1dc in first tr, 2ch, 1tr in each of next 2tr, [3ch, 3tr in next 3ch sp] 3 times, 3ch, * using B, 3tr in foll 3ch sp, 3ch, 3tr in next 3ch sp, using A, [3ch, 3tr in next 3ch sp] 6 times, 3ch, rep from * 2 more times, using B, 3tr in next 3ch sp, 3ch, 3tr in foll 3ch sp, using A, [3ch, 3tr in next 3ch sp] 3 times. 3ch, 1tr in each of last 3 sts.

2nd and 3rd rows form the 3tr and 3ch sp patt and set position of 4 diamonds in B. Cont in patt from chart, changing colours as indicated and noting that the 3ch at each side of the diamonds in B are always worked in A or C, work 4th to 24th rows, then 9th to 24th rows and 25th to 32nd rows, making 45 more rows in all, so completing 3rd line of diamonds in B.
Patt 1 row in A.
Fasten off.

Overchecks
With WS facing, join D in starting chain as indicated on chart, work 3ch, ss in next row diagonally across each 3ch space to last row. Fasten off.
Work all the diagonals in one direction first, then work the diagonals in the other direction substituting 1ch, ss over ch in D, 1ch, when the overchecks cross.

edging

With WS facing, join A between 2nd and 3rd tr at end of first row.

1st round (WS): Working over first 2 sts each time, * [2dc in each row-end] to corner, 3ch, 2dc in same corner row-end, [2dc in 3ch sp, 1dc between each of next 2tr] to last sp, 2dc in last sp, 2dc between next 2 sts at corner, 3ch, rep from * to end, ss in first dc, turn.

2nd round: Ss in 3ch sp, 1ch, * [1dc, 3ch, 1dc] in corner 3ch sp, [1dc in each dc] to next corner, rep from * to end, ss in first dc.

3rd round: 1ch, * 1dc in each dc to corner, [1dc, 3ch, 1dc] in corner 3ch sp, rep from * to end, ss in first dc, turn.

4th round: As 2nd round.

Fasten off.

to make up

Press according to ball band. Darn in ends.

key

A

B

C

overcheck in D

each square in colour
represents 3tr

each uncoloured
square represents a
3ch sp

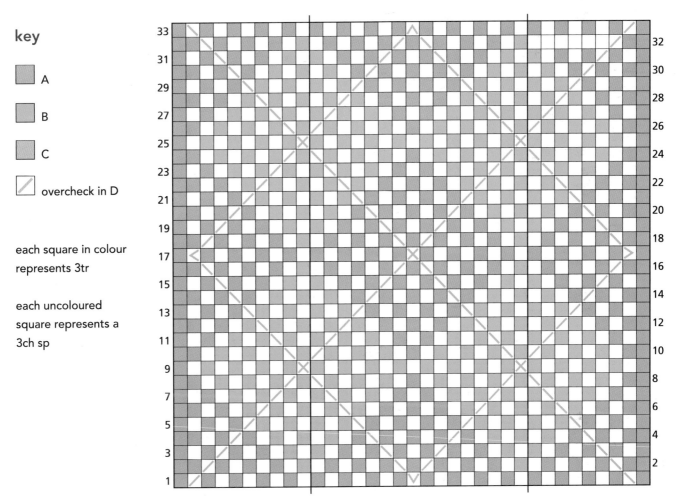

gingham *blanket*

Here, the classic three-colour gingham check fabric is interpreted in a simple crochet design to make a sweet little blanket.

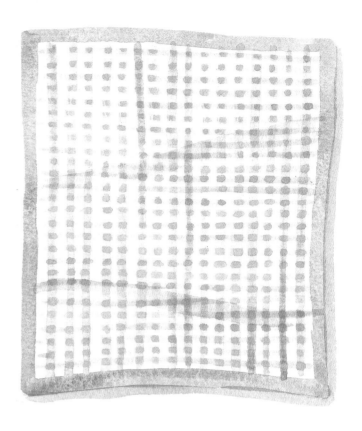

SIZE
63 x 68cm (24¾ x 26¾in)

YOU WILL NEED
3 x 50g balls of Sublime Extra Fine Merino DK in bright blue (A)
3 x 50g balls same in pale blue (B)
2 x 50g balls same in cream (C)
4.00mm (US F/5) crochet hook

TENSION
18 sts and 9 rows to 10cm (4in) over gingham check treble patt, using 4.00mm (US F/5) hook. Change hook size, if necessary, to obtain this tension.

ABBREVIATIONS
ch = chain; **dc** = double crochet; **patt** = pattern; **rep** = repeat; **RS** = right side; **sp** = space; **ss** = slip stitch; **st(s)** = stitch(es); **tr** = treble; **WS** = wrong side; [ ] = work instructions in square brackets as directed.

NOTES
• When changing colours, always pull through the last loop of the last stitch before the colour change with the new colour.
• When working the check pattern, lay yarn colour not in use on top of next 3 sts, (or 4 at each end of the row) and work over it ready to pick it up and change colours.
• Save time by working over the ends of the C yarn, then darn the ends of the A yarn into the border.

blanket

Using A, make 102ch.
1st row (WS): Working into strand at back of ch each time, 1dc in 2nd ch from hook, [1dc in each ch] to end. 101 sts.
2nd row: Using C, 1dc in first dc, 2ch, 1tr in each of next 3dc, [using B, 1tr in each of foll 3dc, using C, 1tr in each of next 3dc] 16 times, 1tr in last dc. Fasten off C.
3rd row: Using B, 1dc in first tr, 2ch, 1tr in each of next 3tr, [using A, 1tr in each of foll 3tr, using B, 1tr in each of next 3tr] 16 times, 1tr in 2nd ch.
Fasten off A.
4th row: Using C, 1dc in first tr, 2ch, 1tr in each of next 3tr, [using B, 1tr in each of foll 3tr, using C, 1tr in each of next 3tr] 16 times, 1tr in 2nd ch.
Fasten off C.
3rd and 4th rows form the gingham check tr patt.
Cont in patt, work 52 more rows, so ending with a 4th row.
Last row (WS): Using A, 1ch, [1dc in each tr] to end.
Fasten off.
With RS facing, join A between first 2 sts of first gingham check tr row at lower right corner.
1st side foundation row (RS): 1dc between first 2 sts of same row as join, [1ch, 1dc between first 2 sts of next row] to end.
Next row: 1ch, 1dc in first dc, [1dc in next 1ch sp, 1dc in next dc] to end. Fasten off.

2nd side foundation row: With RS facing, join A between first 2 sts of last gingham check tr row at top left corner, complete as first side but do not fasten off, turn.

border

1st round (RS): 1ch, 1dc in first dc, [1dc in each dc to corner, 2ch] 4 times, ss in first dc, turn.
2nd round: Ss in corner 2ch sp, 1ch, * [1dc, 2ch, 1dc] in 2ch sp, [1dc in each dc] to next corner, rep from * to end, ss in first dc, ss in 2ch sp, turn.
3rd round: 1ch, 1dc in 2ch sp, * [1dc in each dc] to corner, [1dc, 2ch, 1dc] in 2ch sp, rep from * to end omitting last dc, ss in first dc, turn.
Work 2nd and 3rd rounds one more time, then work 2nd round again. Fasten off.

to make up

Press according to ball band. Darn in ends.

chapter 2 *american dream*

shaker-style *throw*

Easy-to-work treble squares in soft, homespun effect natural fibre yarn give this throw simple, subtle style. You can't go wrong with matching and blending the colours; just choose a shaded yarn and as you work each square will appear to be a slightly different colour.

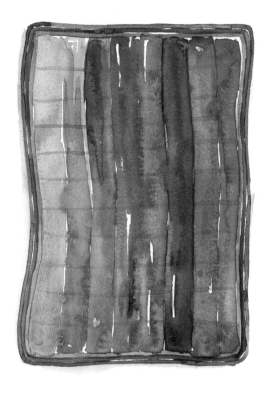

SIZE
64 x 85cm (25¼ x 33½in)

YOU WILL NEED
7 x 50g balls of silk, mohair and wool mix Aran weight yarn in random shaded grey
5.50mm (US I/9) crochet hook

TENSION
Each square measures 7 x 7cm (2¾ x 2¾in), when pressed, using 5.50mm (US I/9) hook. Change hook size, if necessary, to obtain this size square.

ABBREVIATIONS
ch = chain; **dc** = double crochet; **rep** = repeat; **RS** = right side; **sp** = space; **ss** = slip stitch; **tr** = treble; **WS** = wrong side; **[ ]** = work instructions in square brackets as directed.

NOTES
• Sort the squares in piles of different colours and try out different arrangements of the colours before joining the squares.
• When arranging the squares place each square with the end of the 2nd round pointing in the same direction.
• Work the joining dc loosely.

square

Wind yarn around finger to form a ring.
1st round (RS): 1ch, 1dc in ring, 4ch, [3tr in ring, 2ch] 3 times, 2tr in ring, ss in 2nd ch.
2nd round: Ss in 2ch sp, 1ch, [1dc, 4ch, 1tr] in same 2ch sp, * 1tr in each of next 3tr, [1tr, 2ch, 1tr] in next 2ch sp, rep from * two more times, 1tr in each of next 3tr, ss in 2nd ch.
Fasten off.

blanket

Make 88 squares. The shaded yarn will make it appear that the squares are different shades and colours. Arranging colours as wished, place squares in 8 lines of 11 squares.

join squares

With RS of first square of first line and first square of 2nd line together, join yarn in corner 2ch sp of both squares together, 1ch, 1dc in both 2ch sps together, [1dc in next st of both squares together] 5 times, 1dc in next 2ch sps together, [1ch, join next 2 squares in the same way] 10 times.
Fasten off.

Making sure that chains between squares are not twisted when joining 3rd line to 2nd line, join next 6 lines of squares in the same way.
Turn work and join squares in the other direction in the same way.

edging

With RS facing, join yarn in 2ch sp at one corner.
1st round: 1ch, 1dc in same place as join, * [2ch, 1dc] in same 2ch sp, 1dc in each of next 5 sts, [1dc in next 2ch sp, 1dc over dc join, 1dc in foll 2ch sp, 1dc in each of next 5 sts] to corner, 1dc in corner 2ch sp, rep from * along each side omitting last dc, ss in first dc.
2nd round: Ss in first 2ch sp, [1ch, 1dc, 4ch, 1tr] in same 2ch sp, * 1tr in each dc to corner, [1tr, 2ch, 1tr] in 2ch sp, rep from * two more times, 1tr in each dc to corner, ss in 2nd ch.
3rd round: As 2nd round but working into tr, turn.
4th round: 1ch, * 1dc in each tr to corner, [1dc, 2ch, 1dc] in corner 2ch sp, rep from * 3 more times, ss in first dc.
Fasten off.

to make up

Darn in ends. Press lightly on WS.

navajo *blanket*

The centre star with its radiating saw-tooth borders motif is inspired by a Navajo Eyedazzler blanket pattern. Although it looks complicated, actually it's made with just little stepped-edge squares in double crochet worked out from the centre to give two triangles in different colours.

SIZE
74 x 97cm (29 x 38in)

YOU WILL NEED
7 x 50g balls of pure wool Aran weight yarn in brown (A)
1 x 50g ball same in duck egg (B)
4 x 50g balls same in cream (C)
2 x 50g balls same in each of stone (D); dusty pink (E) and dark turquoise (F)
6.00mm (US J/10) crochet hook

TENSION
Each double triangle square measures 12cm (4¾in) across from corner to corner. Change hook size, if necessary, to obtain this size square.

ABBREVIATIONS
ch = chain; **dc** = double crochet; **RS** = right side; **st(s)** = stitch(es); **WS** = wrong side; **[ ]** = work instructions in square brackets as directed.

NOTE
• To save darning in ends and joining yarn for sewing up, simply leave ends long enough to join the squares.

double triangle square
First triangle
Using first colour, make 16ch.
1st row (WS): 1dc in 2nd ch from hook, [1dc in each ch] to end. 15 sts.
2nd row: 2ch, miss first dc, 1dc in each of next 13dc, turn. 13 sts.
3rd row: 2ch, miss first dc, 1dc in each of next 11dc, turn. 11 sts.
4th row: 2ch, miss first dc, 1dc in each of next 9dc, turn. 9 sts.
5th row: 2ch, miss first dc, 1dc in each of next 7dc, turn. 7 sts.
6th row: 2ch, miss first dc, 1dc in each of next 5 sts, turn. 5 sts.
7th row: 2ch, miss first dc, 1dc in each of next 3 sts, turn. 3 sts.
8th row: 2ch, miss first dc, 1dc in next dc.
Fasten off.
2nd triangle
With WS facing join 2nd colour in base of first ch.
1st row: 1ch, [1dc in base of each ch] to end. 15 sts.
Complete as given for first triangle.

blanket
Squares
Make one square using A for both colours, 6 squares using B for first colour and C for 2nd colour, 2 using B for both colours, 14 using A for first colour and D for 2nd colour, 2 using D for both colours, 22 using E for first colour and C for 2nd colour, 16 using A for first colour and C for 2nd colour and 8 using F for first colour and C for 2nd colour.
Triangles
Following instructions for first triangle only, make 4 triangles in F and 22 in A.

join squares and triangles
All squares are sewn together with the starting chain running horizontally. Place the brown square in the centre.
1st outline: Placing cream next to the centre square, sew 3 duck

egg and cream squares above and 3 below, then fill in at each side with a duck egg square.

2nd outline: Placing brown next to duck egg, sew 7 brown and stone squares above and below and one stone square at each side.

3rd outline: Placing dusty pink next to stone, sew 11 dusty pink and cream squares above and below, fill in at each side with a brown triangle placing the chain edge vertically.

4th outline: Placing brown next to cream, sew 4 brown and cream squares in each quarter, filling in at sides with triangles in dark turquoise placed vertically and at top and lower edge with triangles in brown placed horizontally.

5th outline: Placing dark turquoise next to cream, sew 2 dark turquoise and cream squares in each quarter, filling in at sides, top and lower edge with triangles in brown, then sew two triangles in each corner.

border

Upper border

Using A and with WS facing, join yarn in base of first ch of corner triangle.

1st row: 1ch, 1dc in base of each of first 15ch, [1dc in contrast dc between triangles, 1dc in base of each of next 15ch] 5 times. 95 sts.

2nd row: 1ch, [1dc in each dc] to end. 2nd row forms dc.

Cont in dc, work 1 more row in A, 3 rows in F and 4 rows in A. Fasten off.

Lower border

Using A and with WS facing join yarn in base of first ch of corner triangle. Complete as upper border.

Side edgings

Using A and with WS facing join yarn in last row-end of lower border.

1st row: 1ch, 1dc in each of next 10 row-ends, 1dc in base of corner ch of lower border triangle, [1dc in base of each of next 15ch, 1dc in each of next 2 row-ends] 6 times, 1dc in base of each of next 15ch, 1dc in base of corner ch of upper border triangle, 1dc in each of next 10 row-ends. 139 sts.

Turn and work 1 row dc.

Fasten off.

to make up

Darn in ends. Press on WS.

make a navajo-style cushion

Make just the centre outlined star motif for a front to fit a 50 x 50cm (19½ x 19½in) square cushion. You'll need 1 x 50g ball of pure wool Aran weight yarn in each of the first four colours listed.

Squares

Make one square using A for both colours, 6 squares using B for first colour and C for 2nd colour, 2 using B for both colours, 12 using A for first colour and D for 2nd colour and 4 using A for first colour and C for 2nd colour.

Triangles

Make 6 triangles in A, 4 in B and 2 in D.

Small triangles

Make 4 in A. Make 10 ch. Missing first ch, work [1dc in each ch] to end. 9 sts. Complete as first triangle from 5th row.

To make up

Assemble squares in same way as centre motif of blanket, filling in at top and lower edge with triangles in A and at sides with triangles in D and B, finish the corners with small triangles in A. Work one or two rounds of dc in A to finish the edges.

seminole-style *blanket*

This boldly patterned blanket looks like an abstract painting, but it is based on the geometric patchwork designs originally created with ribbons, and later with folded fabric, by the Seminole of Florida.

SIZE
95 x 112cm (37½ x 44in)

YOU WILL NEED
10 x 50g balls of pure wool DK in navy (A)
2 x 50g balls same in each of magenta (B) and lime green (C)
6.00mm (US J/10) crochet hook

TENSION
Each flying diamond strip measures 9 x 32cm (3½ x 12½in), joins measure 1cm (⅜in), each panel of eight strips measures 32 x 79cm (12½ x 31in), vertical strips measure 4 x 79cm (1½in x 31in), horizontal strips measure 8 x 80cm (3⅛in x 31½in), border measures 7.5cm (3in), all using 6.00mm (US J/10) hook. Change hook size, if necessary, to obtain these sizes.

ABBREVIATIONS
ch = chain; **cont** = continue; **dc** = double crochet; **2dctog** = insert hook in first st and pull loop through, insert hook in 2nd st and pull loop through, yarn around hook and pull through 3 loops on hook; **dec** = decreasing; **patt** = pattern; **RS** = right side; **ss** = slip stitch; **st(s)** = stitch(es); **WS** = wrong side; [ ] = work instructions in square brackets as directed.

NOTES
• When working the flying diamond strips, the chain at the start of a row is counted as a stitch.
• When assembling the strips, make sure that you have the correct number of dc along each edge or part of an edge to match the stitches when working the joins.

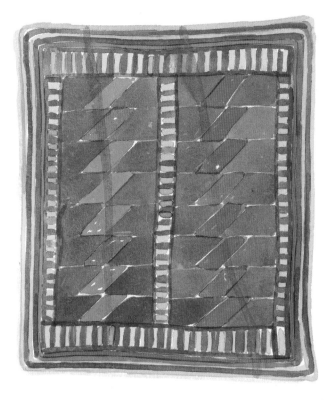

flying diamond strips panel
First flying diamond strip
Using A, make 2ch.
Increase from corner
1st row: 2dc in 2nd ch from hook.
2nd row: 1ch, 1dc in first dc, 1dc in next dc, 2dc in end ch. 5 sts.
3rd row: 1ch, 1dc in first dc, 1dc in each dc, 2dc in end ch. 7 sts.
3rd row forms dc with one st increased at each end.
Work 6 more rows in same way as 3rd row. 19 sts.
Work straight
10th row: 1ch, miss first dc, 2dctog, 1dc in each dc, 2dc in end ch. 19 sts.
11th row: 1ch, 1dc in first dc, 1dc in each dc, miss end ch, turn. 19 sts.
10th and 11th rows form dc on the diagonal.
Work 10th and 11th rows 3 more times, then work 10th row again. Change to B.
Next row (RS): Work as 11th row.
Cont in B, work 10th and 11th rows 4 more times.
Change to A, work 10th and 11th rows 4 more times, then work 10th row again.

Decrease to corner

1st row: 1ch, miss first dc, 2dctog, 1dc in each dc, miss end ch, turn. Cont in dc, dec in this way on every row until 3 sts remain.

Next row: 1ch, 1dc in 2dctog, do not turn.

Lower edging row: With RS of strip facing work 1ch, 17dc in row-ends of longer section in A, 9dc in row-ends in B and 9dc in row-ends of shorter section in A. Fasten off.

2nd flying diamond strip

Work as given for first flying diamond strip.

Upper edging row: With RS facing, join A in top right corner, work as given for lower edging row.

Fasten off.

joining row

With WS together and RS of 2nd flying diamond strip facing, join upper edging row of 2nd flying diamond strip to lower edging row of first flying diamond strip. Using A make 1ch, working loosely, insert hook under first dc of each edge, catch yarn and pull loop through sts and loop on hook, cont in this way until all sts are joined.

Fasten off.

3rd, 4th, 5th, 6th and 7th flying diamond strips

Work as 2nd flying diamond strip, joining each upper edging row to lower edging row of previous strip.

8th flying diamond strip

Work as first flying diamond strip omitting lower edging row. Work upper edging row as 2nd flying diamond strip and join to lower edging row of 7th strip.

Work 2nd flying diamond strips panel in the same way.

vertical strips

1st vertical strip

Using A, make 6ch.

1st row (WS): 1dc in 2nd ch from hook, [1dc in each ch] to end. 6 sts.

2nd row: 1ch, miss first dc, 1dc in each dc, 1dc in end ch. 2nd row forms dc.

Cont in stripe patt of 2 rows C, 4 rows A, until 21 stripes in C have been completed. Work 2 more rows A, do not fasten off.

1st edging row: With RS facing, work 1ch, 105 dc evenly in row-ends along edge of strip. Fasten off.

2nd edging row: Join A in opposite corner and work as first edging row. Fasten off.

Make 2 more vertical strips in the same way.

tip

To work double crochet evenly along the row-ends of the striped strips, work 1dc in each row-end in A and 1dc in each 2 row ends in C.

join flying diamond panels and vertical strips

Join A in top right corner of first flying diamond panel, work 13dc in row-ends of first vertical strip, [1dc in join, 12dc in row-ends of next strip] 7 times, 1dc in end ch. 105 sts.

Join A in lower left corner of same panel and finish the other side edge in the same way.

Edge 2nd panel in the same way.

Join vertical strip between panels and at each side in same way as joining flying diamond panels.

horizontal strips

1st horizontal strip

Using A, make 12ch.

1st row (WS): 1dc in 2nd ch from hook, [1dc in each ch] to end. 12 sts.

Cont in dc, work 1 more row A, then work in stripe patt as given for vertical strips until 22nd stripe in C has been completed. Work 2 more rows A, do not fasten off.

1st edging row: With RS facing, work 1ch, 110dc evenly in row-ends along edge of strip.

Fasten off.

2nd edging row: Join A in opposite corner and work as first edging row.

Fasten off.

Make 2nd horizontal strip in the same way.

join horizontal strips

Join A in top right corner of right vertical strip and work 110dc evenly along top edge of vertical strips and panels.

Fasten off.

Join A in lower left corner of left vertical strip and finish lower edge in the same way.

Join horizontal strips to upper and lower edges of blanket in same way as joining flying diamond panels.

border

With RS facing, join A at centre of lower edge.

1st round: 1ch, [1dc in each dc or join to corner, 3dc in corner] 4 times, [1dc in each dc] to end, ss in first dc, turn.

Cont in dc, working 3dc in each corner dc and turning at the end of each round, work 1 more round in A, 2 rounds B, 3 rounds A, 2 rounds C, 3 rounds A and 1 round C.

Fasten off.

to make up

Darn in ends. Press lightly on WS.

make a bigger throw

For a longer throw

Add more flying diamond strips to each panel. Each extra joined panel will increase the length by 10cm (4in). Adjust the length of the vertical strips and edging rows to fit.

For a wider throw

Add more flying diamond strips panels. Each extra panel will need another vertical strip to join it to the previous panels increasing the width by 38cm (15in). If you make a bigger throw, you will need more yarn.

sunshine & shadow *throw*

This stunning throw is in the style of an Amish patchwork quilt. It's made from very simple little squares of crochet in alternating bright, dark and light colours arranged to make a diamond design and finished with a bold border.

SIZE
117 x 117cm (46 x 46in)

YOU WILL NEED
Approximately:
270g pure wool or wool rich DK yarn in black (A)
65g same in red (B)
50g same in lime (C)
100g same in magenta (D)
50g same in lilac (E)
100g same in dark turquoise (F)
50g same in bright turquoise (G)
65g same in purple (H)
200g same in dull purple (I)
4.00mm (US F/5) crochet hook

TENSION
Each square measures approximately 5.25 x 5.25cm (just over 2 x 2in), 17 squares x 17 squares measures 89cm (35in), corner squares measure 11.5 x 11.5cm (4½ x 4½in), all using 4mm (US F/5) hook. Change hook size, if necessary, to obtain this size squares.

ABBREVIATIONS
ch = chain; **dc** = double crochet; **dtr** = double treble; **foll** = following; **tr** = treble; **rep** = repeat; **RS** = right side; **sp** = space; **ss** = slip stitch; **st(s)** = stitch(es); **WS** = wrong side; **[ ]** = work instructions in square brackets as directed.

NOTES
• Yarn amounts are approximate because the amount of squares that can be made from a 50g ball of yarn varies between 24 and 28 depending on brand and the fibre content.
• The size of the squares averages out to 5.25 x 5.25cm (just over 2 x 2in) but, again depending on the yarn used, may measure between 5 x 5cm (2 x 2in) and 5.5 x 5.5cm (2⅛ x 2⅛in).

throw
Centre square
Wind A around finger to form a ring.
1st round (RS): 4ch, [3tr, 1ch] 3 times in ring, 2tr in ring, ss in 3rd ch.
2nd round: Ss in 1ch sp, 5ch, 1dtr in same 1ch sp, * 2tr in next tr, 1tr in foll tr, 2tr in next tr, [1dtr, 1ch, 1dtr] in 1ch sp, rep from * two more times, 2tr in next tr, 1tr in foll tr, 2tr in last tr, ss in 4th ch. Fasten off.
1st ring of squares: Make 4 squares in B, joining each square to centre square in A to form a cross shape by working 1dc in 1ch sp of centre square instead of 1ch between dtr at two of the corners.
2nd ring of squares: Make 8 squares in C, joining first square to top 2 corners of top square in B, continuing clockwise join 2nd corner of next square to top corner of same square in B, 3rd corner to centre square in A and 4th corner to top corner of next square in B; 2 corners of foll square to outer corners of next square in B, next square in same way as 2nd square and next square to lower corners of next square in B, continue in this way until all 2nd ring squares are made and joined
Following diagram, continue joining squares with 2 corners at top, lower edge and at each side and to adjacent corners in between in this way.
3rd ring of squares: Make and join 12 squares in B.
4th ring of squares: Make and join 16 squares in A.
5th ring of squares: Make and join 20 squares in D.
6th ring of squares: Make and join 24 squares in E.
7th ring of squares: Make and join 28 squares in D.
8th ring of squares: Make and join 32 squares in A.
Fill in corners with lines of squares.
1st line of squares: Make and join 8 squares in F at each corner.

2nd line of squares: Make and join 7 squares in G at each corner.
3rd line of squares: Make and join 6 squares in F at each corner.
4th line of squares: Make and join 5 squares in A at each corner.
5th line of squares: Make and join 4 squares in H at each corner.
6th line of squares: Make and join 3 squares in C at each corner.
7th line of squares: Make and join 2 squares in H at each corner.
Fill in each corner with a square in A.
Join all squares by over sewing them on WS so chain edges of 2nd round show on RS. Press lightly on WS.

borders

With RS facing, join A in a corner 1ch sp.
1st row: 1ch, 1dc in same place as join, 2ch, work 1tr in each st and each 1ch sp to next corner. Fasten off.
With RS facing, join I in 2nd ch at start of first row.
2nd row: 1ch, 1dc in same place as join, 2ch, [1tr in each tr] to end. Turning each time, work 6 more rows in tr. Fasten off.
Finish remaining 3 sides in the same way.

corner squares

Using B, work as centre square until 2 rounds have been completed, do not fasten off.
3rd round: Ss in 1ch sp, 5ch, 1dtr in same 1ch sp, * 2tr in next dtr, 1tr in each of foll 5tr, 2tr in next dtr **, [1dtr, 1ch, 1dtr] in 1ch sp, rep from * two more times, then rep from * to **, ss in 4th ch.
4th round: Ss in 1ch sp, 5ch, 1dtr in same 1ch sp, * 2tr in next dtr, 1tr in each of foll 9tr, 2tr in next dtr **, [1dtr, 1ch, 1dtr] in 1ch sp, rep from * two more times joining last corner with a dc to corner 1ch sp of centre, then rep from * to **, ss in 4th ch.
Fasten off.
Make and join 3 more squares, one for each corner, in this way.
With chain edge of 4th round showing on RS, join sides of squares to row-ends of borders by over sewing on WS.

edging

Join A in a corner 1ch sp of a corner square in B.
1st round: [5ch, 1dtr in same sp as join, * 2tr in dtr, [1tr in each tr] to st before next corner, 2tr in this st **, [1dtr, 1ch, 1dtr] in corner 1ch sp, rep from * two more times, then rep from * to **, ss in 4th ch.
2nd round: Ss in first 1ch sp, [1dtr, 1ch, 1dtr] in same 1ch sp, complete as first round, turn.
3rd round: 1ch, 1dc in same place as ss, [1dc in each st to corner, 4dc in corner 1ch sp] 4 times, ss in first dc.
Fasten off.

to make up

Darn in ends. Press lightly on WS.

tips

• The squares are joined as they are made because this helps keep track of how many to make in each colour and stops them getting lost. Leave long ends and sew them up as you work.

• If you prefer you could make the squares separately and join them in the order given when sewing up.

• You could use several shades of each of the colours listed.

• If you think you are going to run out of a colour, work in from each edge when joining squares, then if you need to use a different colour the balance of colours will be the same in each section.

• If you are really stuck for matching a colour, you may be able to find the right shade in tapestry wool.

• If you want to invent your own colour scheme, use the yarn amounts given as a guide. If you want the shaded effect, make sure that you keep the same balance of dark, medium and light tones.

diagram for assembling squares

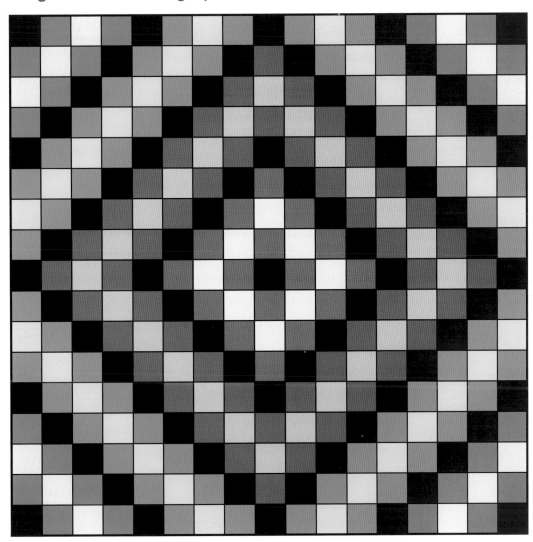

log cabin *coverlet*

Here, the traditional log cabin patchwork, which is made by sewing strips around a centre square of fabric, is interpreted in crochet by carefully arranged colour changes in a simple square motif. For this coverlet, the squares have been assembled in a pattern known as Straight Furrow but check out old quilt patterns for other ways of creating designs with this motif.

SIZE
56.5 x 73.5cm (22¼ x 29in)

YOU WILL NEED
Approximately:
100g of cotton DK yarn in soft red (A)
30g same in each of taupe (B) and pale yellow (C)
40g same in each of soft orange (D) and cream (E)
50g same in each of black (F) and bright yellow (G)
4.50mm (US G/6) crochet hook

TENSION
Each square measures 15.5 x 15.5cm
(6 x 6in), using 4.50mm (US G/6) hook. Change
hook size, if necessary, to obtain
this size square.

ABBREVIATIONS
ch = chain; **dc** = double crochet; **rep** = repeat;
RS = right side; **sp** = space; **ss** = slip stitch;
st(s) = stitch(es); **tr** = treble; **[ ]** = work instructions
in square brackets as directed.

log cabin square

Using A, wind yarn around finger to form a ring.
1st round (RS): 1ch, 1dc in ring, 4ch, [3tr in ring, 2ch] 3 times, 2tr in ring, ss in 2nd ch, ss in 2ch sp, turn.
2nd round: 1ch, 1dc in corner sp, * 1dc in each of next 3tr, [1dc, 2ch, 1dc] in next corner sp, rep from * 2 more times, 1dc in each of last 3tr, 1dc in first corner sp, 2ch, ss in first dc.
Fasten off.
With RS facing, join B in first corner sp.
3rd round: 1ch, 1dc in same place as join, 4ch, ss in 3rd ch from hook (this stands as first ch of first corner sp), * 1tr in each of next 5dc, [1tr, 2ch, 1tr] in next corner sp, 1tr in each of foll 5dc, 1tr in next corner sp, 1ch *, change to C, 1ch, 1tr in same corner ch, rep from * to * once more, ss in corner ch, taking yarn in front of hook, turn.
4th round: Cont in C, 3ch, ss in 2nd ch from hook (this stands as first ch of first corner sp), 1dc in first corner sp, * 1dc in each of next 7tr, [1dc, 2ch, 1dc] in next corner sp, 1dc in each of foll 7tr, 1dc in next corner sp, 1ch *, change to B, taking hook under strand 1ch, 1dc in same corner sp, rep from * to * once more, ss in corner ch.
Fasten off.
With RS facing, join D in first corner sp.

5th round: 1ch, 1dc in same place as join, 4ch, ss in 3rd ch from hook, * 1tr in each of next 9dc, [1tr, 2ch, 1tr] in next corner sp, 1tr in each of foll 9dc, 1tr in next corner sp, 1ch *, change to E, 1ch, 1tr in same corner sp, rep from * to * once more, ss in corner ch, taking yarn in front of hook, turn.

6th round: Cont in E, 3ch, ss in 2nd ch from hook, 1dc in first corner sp, * 1dc in each of next 11tr, [1dc, 2ch, 1dc] in next corner sp, 1dc in each of foll 11tr, 1dc in next corner sp, 1ch *, change to D, taking hook under strand 1ch, 1dc in same corner sp, rep from * to * once more, ss in corner ch.
Fasten off.
With RS facing, join F in first corner sp.

7th round: 1ch, 1dc in same place as join, 4ch, ss in 3rd ch from hook, * 1tr in each of next 13dc, [1tr, 2ch, 1tr] in next corner sp, 1tr in each of foll 13dc, 1tr in next corner sp, 1ch *, change to G, 1ch, 1tr in same corner sp, rep from * to * once more, ss in corner ch, taking yarn in front of hook, turn.

8th round: Cont in G, 3ch, ss in 2nd ch from hook, 1dc in first corner sp, * 1dc in each of next 15tr, [1dc, 2ch, 1dc] in next corner sp, 1dc in each of foll 15tr, 1dc in next corner sp, 1ch *, change to F, taking hook under strand 1ch, 1dc in same corner sp, rep from * to * once more, 1ch, ss in corner sp.
Fasten off.

coverlet

Make 12 log cabin squares.

Join squares

With RS facing, arrange squares in an oblong 3 squares wide and 4 squares down starting with a dark section at top left of first square on the left and alternating light and dark to form a diagonal pattern. Join squares in a zigzag, using G, join yarn in right corner sp of centre square at lower edge, 1ch, 1dc in same sp, 1ch, 1dc in corresponding sp of adjacent square on the right, 1ch, miss 1dc of centre square, 1dc in next dc, 1ch, 1dc in corresponding dc of adjacent square, continue in this way until edges are joined, ending with 1ch, 1dc in next corner sp of centre square, 1ch, 1dc in corresponding corner sp of adjacent square, continue joining square on lower right to square above it in the same way. Fasten off after last dc in corner sp.

For the 2nd join, use F and work in a zigzag in the same way as first join, working 1ch, ss in dc at opposite corner, 1ch, 1dc in same 2ch sp as last dc to join corners between joining edges of squares. Using F or G as appropriate, continue until all squares are joined.

border

With RS facing, join A in lower right corner sp.

1st round: 1ch, [1dc, 4ch, 1tr] in corner sp, * [1tr in each of next 17dc, 1tr in next 2 ch sp, 2tr in join between squares, 1tr in 2ch sp of next square] 3 times, 1dc in each of next 17dc, [1tr, 2ch, 1tr] in corner 2ch sp, [1tr in each of next 17dc, 1tr in 2ch sp, 2tr in join between squares, 1tr in 2ch sp of next square] twice, 1tr in each of next 17dc *, [1tr, 2ch, 1tr] in corner 2ch sp, rep from * to * once more, ss in 2nd ch, ss in corner sp, turn.

2nd round: 1ch, 1dc in 2ch sp, * 1dc in each dc to corner, [1dc, 2ch, 1dc] in corner sp, rep from * to end omitting last dc, ss in first dc, turn.

3rd round: 1ch, [1dc, 4ch, 1tr] in corner sp, * 1tr in each dc to next corner, [1tr, 2ch, 1tr] in corner sp, rep from * 2 more times, 1tr in each dc to corner, ss in 2nd ch, ss in corner sp, turn.

4th round: As 2nd round.

Fasten off.

to make up

Press on WS. Darn in ends.

SIZE
57 x 76cm (22½ x 30in)

YOU WILL NEED
Approximately 170g of DK yarn in a mix of colours: 25g each in fuchsia alpaca, lime bamboo, red silk mix and yellow bamboo, 20g each in orange silk and pale lime silk, 10g each in purple mohair, bright pink mohair and lilac mohair (A)
Approximately 110g pure wool DK in black (B)
4.00mm (US F/5) crochet hook
6 buttons

TENSION
Each square measures 15 x 15cm (6 x 6in) before edging, 19 x 19cm (7½ x 7½in) after edging, using 4.00mm (US F/5) hook. Change hook size, if necessary, to obtain this size square.

ABBREVIATIONS
ch = chain; **dc** = double crochet; **2dctog** = insert hook in first sp and pull loop through, insert hook in 2nd sp and pull loop through, yarn around hook and pull through 3 loops on hook; **rep** = repeat; **RS** = right side; **sp(s)** = space(s); **ss** = slip stitch; **st(s)** = stitch(es); **tr** = treble; **WS** = wrong side; **[ ]** = work instructions in square brackets as directed.

NOTES
• This is where you raid your stash for all those unusual yarns you've been hoarding but couldn't find a use for. The yarn amounts given are those used to make the throw in the picture.
• You may use any kind of yarn you want as long as it is roughly a double knitting weight but bear in mind that different fibre yarns may require different amounts to complete the throw.
• Each square is made up of 4 shapes and 2 flowers. For the original the motifs have been assembled in the same way for each square, only the colours and yarn textures are varied. If you want, you can play around with the arrangement, substitute more flowers for the leaf spray or even invent motifs of your own, but best to make at least one square first exactly as given to be sure that you have the same number of spaces as the original along the edges so your squares will fit together.
• When working the motifs, leave long ends and use them to sew the pieces together.
• When arranging the motifs don't put all the motifs in the same yarn together; instead, you can compensate for the fact that the sizes may vary slightly, depending on the type of yarn used, by joining larger and smaller motifs to give an average size square.

crazy patchwork *throw*

From the 1880s onward there was a great craze for making decorative patchwork using even the tiniest random-shaped scraps of silk, satin and velvet. This crochet version of crazy patchwork is the ultimate in scrap yarn designs, with its richly coloured, contrasting texture shapes combined to make exciting patterned squares. Vary the colours so each square is different then join them with black to make a dramatic throw.

motifs
Top left mesh
Make 20ch.

1st row (RS): Working into back strand of each ch, 1tr in 6th ch from hook, [1ch, miss 1ch, 1tr in next ch] 7 times.

2nd row: 1dc in first tr, 3ch, [1tr in next tr, 1ch] 7 times, miss 1ch, 1tr in next ch.

3rd row: As 2nd row.

4th row: 1dc in first tr, 3ch, 1tr in next tr, turn.

5th row: 1dc in first tr, 3ch, miss 1ch, 1tr in next ch.

6th row: As 5th row.

Fasten off.

Lower right mesh

Note that first row is a WS row. Work as given for top left mesh until 2nd row has been completed. Work 4th row, then work 5th row 4 times.
Fasten off.

Lower left fan

Make 6ch, ss in first ch to form a ring.
1st row (RS): 1ch, 1dc in ring, 3ch, 1tr in ring, [1ch, 1tr in ring] twice.
2nd row: 1dc in first tr, 3ch, [1tr in next 1ch sp, 1ch] 3 times, 1tr in 2nd ch.
3rd row: 1dc in first tr, 3ch, 1tr in next 1ch sp, 1ch, [1tr, 1ch] twice in each of next two 1ch sps, 1tr in last 1ch sp, 1ch, 1tr in 2nd ch.
4th row: 1dc in first 1ch sp, [4ch, 1dc in next 1ch sp] 6 times.
Fasten off.

Leaf spray

Make 21ch, ss in 11th ch from hook, turn and work first leaf, 11dc in 11ch sp, ss in same ch as previous ss, turn, miss first dc, 1dc in next dc, [3ch, 1dc in foll dc] 9 times, ss in same ch as previous ss, make 14 ch, ss in 11th ch from hook and work 2nd leaf in same way as first leaf, make 17ch, ss in 11th ch from hook and work 3rd leaf in same way as first leaf, work [3dc, 3ch, 3dc] over 6ch

diagram for assembling motifs

between 3rd and 2nd leaves and [2dc, 3ch, 2dc] over 3ch between 2nd and first leaves, work 3dc over first part of last 10ch, make 11ch, ss in 11th ch from hook and work 4th leaf in same way as first leaf, work 7dc over remaining ch, ss in last ch.
Fasten off.
Note that the round of 3ch loops that complete each leaf are worked with RS facing.

Flower
Make 6ch, ss in first ch to form a ring.
1st round (RS): 1ch, 1dc in ring, [8ch, 1dc in ring] 7 times, 8ch, ss in first dc.
Fasten off.

throw
Using the yarns and colours shown as A as desired, make 12 of each of the first 4 motifs and 24 flowers. Arrange the motifs as shown in diagram and join by stitching adjacent picots and stitches or spaces together to make 12 squares. You can vary the places you join the motifs in the centre but make sure that the spaces along each edge are left free as shown.

edging
With RS facing, join B in corner sp of lower right mesh.
1st round (RS): 1ch, [1dc, 3ch, 1dc] in same sp as join, [1ch, 1dc in next sp of mesh] 7 times, 1ch, 1dc between mesh and top right flower, [1ch, 1dc in next sp of flower] 3 times, 3ch, [1dc in next sp of flower, 1ch] twice, [1dc in next sp of 3rd leaf, 1ch] 4 times, [1dc in next sp of top left mesh, 1ch] 5 times, [1dc, 3ch, 1dc] in corner sp, [1ch, 1dc in next sp of mesh] 6 times, 1ch, placing first part dc in last sp of mesh and 2nd part dc in first sp of fan work 2dctog, 1ch, [1dc in next sp of fan, 1ch] 3 times, [1dc, 3ch, 1dc] in corner sp of fan, [1ch, 1dc in next sp of fan] 3 times, 1ch, 1dc between fan and stem of leaf spray, [1ch, 1dc in next sp of lower right mesh] 6 times, 1ch, ss in first dc.
2nd round: Ss in 3ch sp, 1ch, * [1dc, 3ch, 1dc] in corner 3ch sp, [1dc in next st, 1dc in next 1ch sp] 11 times, 1dc in foll st, rep from * 3 more times, ss in first dc.
3rd round: Ss in corner 3ch sp, 1ch, * [1dc, 3ch, 1dc] in corner 3ch sp, 1dc in next dc, ** 1ch, miss 3dc, [1tr, 1ch] 4 times in foll dc, miss next 3dc, 1dc in foll dc, rep from ** 2 more times, then rep from * 3 more times, ss in first dc. Fasten off.

to make up
Press squares on WS. Sew squares together at the top of the curve of each of the edging shells and, making little bars at the joins, at the corners. Sew a button on each of the centre corner joins.

make a bigger throw
Because the edgings are worked around each square and there isn't a border, you can continue making, edging and joining squares until the throw is the size you want. The amounts for the motifs will vary depending on the yarns you use: for instance, mohair goes a lot further than silk. You'll need to allow an extra 50g ball of pure wool DK in black for every 6 extra squares, plus a little more for the joining the edgings.

chapter 3 *outside inside*

rainbow *baby blanket*

This scrap yarn project echoes the thrifty quilts made by joining narrow strips of fabric. Just collect a rainbow of colours, work them in simple striped strips then join the strips to make a blanket.

SIZE
64 x 89cm (25¼ x 35in)

YOU WILL NEED
Approximately:
60g pure wool or wool-mix DK yarn in shades of red (A)
60g same in shades of orange (B)
40g same in shades of yellow (C)
40g same in shades of green (D)
90g same in shades of blue (E)
40g same in shades of violet (F)
100g same in navy (G)
4.00mm (US F/5) crochet hook

TENSION
21 sts measure 12cm (4¾in) and 12 rows measure 11cm (4¼in) over striped patt, using 4.00mm (US F/5) hook. Change hook size, if necessary, to obtain this tension.

ABBREVIATIONS
ch = chain; **cont** = continue; **dc** = double crochet; **htr** = half treble; **rep** = repeat; **RS** = right side; **sp(s)** = space(s); **ss** = slip stitch; **st(s)** = stitch(es); **tr** = treble; **WS** = wrong side; **[ ]** = work instructions in square brackets as directed.

NOTES
• All yarn amounts are approximate as different brands of yarn vary in length according to the fibre content.
• Use as many shades of each colour as you can find.
• If possible, work each row of each 6-row stripe in a different shade, you'll need just 1½ metres (1⅝ yards) for a dc row and 3 metres (3⅓ yards) for a treble row.
• Work over the ends, leaving any excess yarn on the back of the work to trim off later.
• You'll need almost 50g of one shade of blue for the shell edging.

striped strip

Using a shade of A, make 22ch.
1st row (WS): 1dc in 2nd ch from hook, [1dc in each ch] to end. 21 sts.
Change to 2nd shade of A.
2nd row: 1dc in first dc, 2ch, [1tr in each dc] to end.
Change to 3rd shade of A.
3rd row: 1ch, [1dc in each tr] to last st, 1dc in 2nd ch.
2nd and 3rd rows form the patt.
Changing shades for each row, work 3 more rows A and 6 rows in each of B, C, D, E and F. Starting again with A, cont in 6-row stripes until 85 rows in patt have been completed, so ending with a dc row.
Varying the shades within the stripes, make 3 more striped strips.

join strips

With RS facing, join G in first dc row at lower right corner of first strip.
1st edging row (RS): Inserting hook between 2nd and 3rd sts each time, work 1ch, [1dc, 1htr] in same row as join, * 1ch, miss next tr row, [1htr, 1dc, 1htr] in next dc row-end, rep from * to end omitting last htr. Fasten off.

Join G in last dc row at top left corner of second strip.

2nd edging row: Inserting hook between 2nd and 3rd sts each time, work 1ch, [1dc, 1htr] in same row as join, ss in first 1ch sp at top of 1st edging row, * miss next tr row, [1htr, 1dc, 1htr] in next dc row-end, ss in next 1ch sp of 1st edging row, rep from * to end, 1htr, 1dc in last dc row-end.

Fasten off.

Work 1st edging row up right-hand edge of 2nd strip and 2nd edging row to join 3rd strip to 2nd strip, work 1st edging row up right-hand edge of 3rd strip and 2nd edging row to join 4th strip.

border

With RS facing, join G in first dc row at lower right of 4th strip.

1st round (RS): Inserting hook between 2nd and 3rd sts of row-ends, work up right-hand edge of 4th strip in same way as 1st edging row, ending [1htr, 1dc, 1htr] in last row-end, cont along top edge of joined strips, * 1ch, miss 2dc, [1htr, 1dc, 1htr] in next dc, rep from * 4 more times, 1ch, miss 2dc **, 1htr in same place as edging sts at corner, ss in edging dc at corner of this strip, 1ch, ss in edging dc at corner of next strip, 1htr in same place as edging sts, rep from * 2 more times, then rep from * to **, [1htr, 1dc, 1htr] in corner at top of first strip, work down left-hand edge of first strip in same way as 1st edging row, then work along lower edge in same way as top edge, ending 1htr in same place as first 2 sts, ss in first dc, turn.

2nd round: 1ch, 1dc in same place as ss, missing ch sps unless otherwise directed work * 1dc in each of next 18 sts, [1dc in 1ch sp between strips, 1dc in each of next 19 sts] twice, 1dc in 1ch sp between strips, 1dc in each of next 18 sts, [1dc, 3ch, 1dc] in corner dc, 1dc in each of next 125 sts to corner dc, [1dc, 3ch, 1dc] in corner dc, rep from * along remaining two sides omitting last dc, ss in first dc.

Fasten off.

With RS facing, join A in 3ch sp at lower right, change colours in rainbow order as wished during 3rd round.

3rd round (RS): 1ch, [1dc, 5ch, 1tr] in same 3ch sp as join, 1tr in each of next 127dc, [1tr, 3ch, 1tr] in 3ch sp, 1tr in each of next 79dc, [1tr, 3ch, 1tr] in 3ch sp, 1tr in each of next 127dc, [1tr, 3ch, 1tr] in 3ch sp, 1tr in each of next 79dc, ss in 2nd ch. Fasten off.

With RS facing, join G in 3ch sp at lower right.

4th round (RS): 1ch, * [1dc, 3ch, 1dc] in 3ch sp, 1dc in each of next 129tr, [1dc, 3ch, 1dc] in 3ch sp, 1dc in each of next 81tr, rep from * again, ss in first dc.

5th round: Ss in first 3ch sp, 1ch, [1dc, 5ch, 1tr] in 3ch sp, 1tr in each of next 131dc, [1tr, 3ch, 1tr] in 3ch sp, 1tr in each of next 83dc, [1tr, 3ch, 1tr] in 3ch sp, 1tr in each of next 131dc, [1tr, 3ch, 1tr] in 3ch sp, 1tr in each of next 83dc, ss in 2nd ch.

Fasten off.

With RS facing, join E in first tr at lower right edge.

6th round: 1ch, 1dc in same place as join, * miss 2tr, [3tr, 1ch, 3tr] in next tr, miss 2tr, 1dc in foll tr *, rep from * to * 21 more times up right edge, [3tr, 1ch, 3tr] in 3ch sp, 1dc in next tr, rep from * to * 14 times along top edge, [3tr, 1ch, 3tr] in 3ch sp, 1dc in next tr, rep from * down left edge and along lower edge omitting last dc, ss in first dc. Fasten off.

to make up

Trim worked in ends. Press lightly on WS.

make a bigger blanket

For a blanket that's about 128 x 178cm (50 x 70in), you'll need pure wool or wool-mix DK yarn, approximately: 240g in shades of red (A); 240g in shades of orange (B); 160g in shades of yellow (C); 160g in shades of green (D); 360g in shades of blue (E); 160g in shades of violet (F) and 400g in navy (G).

Striped strips

Make 8 striped strips working in same way as given for baby blanket but completing 169 rows for each strip. Work edgings, joins and borders in same way as baby blanket.

flower garden *throw*

Just like the traditional patchwork design made from flowery print fabric hexagons that's called Grandmother's Flower Garden, this crochet version brings the garden indoors with a boldly patterned throw made from simple flowers surrounded by green leaves.

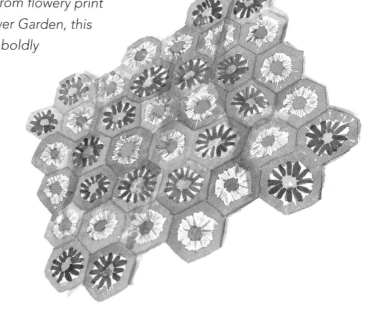

SIZE
75 x 81.5cm (29½ x 32in)

YOU WILL NEED
1 x 50g ball of Debbie Bliss Cashmerino Aran in each of pale green (A), lilac (B) and pink (C)
2 x 50g balls same in white (D)
6 x 50g balls same in grass green (E)
5.50mm (US I/9) crochet hook

TENSION
Each hexagon measures 12.5cm (5in) across from straight side to straight side, 8.5cm (3½in) along a straight side and 14cm (5½in) across from point to point, all using 5.50mm (US I/9) hook. Change hook size, if necessary, to obtain these measurements.

ABBREVIATIONS
ch = chain; **dc** = double crochet; **dtr** = double treble; **2dtrtog** = leaving last loop of each dtr on hook, work 2dtr, yrh and pull through 3 loops on hook; **3dtrtog** = leaving last loop of each dtr on hook, work 3dtr, yrh and pull through 4 loops on hook; **rep** = repeat; **RS** = right side; **sp** = space; **ss** = slip stitch; **tr** = treble; **2trtog** = leaving last loop of each tr on hook, work 2tr, yrh and pull through 3 loops on hook; **3trtog** = leaving last loop of each tr on hook, work 3tr, yrh and pull through 4 loops on hook, **4trtog** = leaving last loop of each tr on hook, work 4tr, yrh and pull though 5 loops on hook; **WS** = wrong side; **yrh** = yarn around hook; **[ ]** = work instructions in square brackets as directed.

flower hexagon
Using A, wind yarn around finger to form a ring.
1st round (RS): 2ch, 2trtog in ring, 2ch, [3trtog, 2ch] 5 times, ss in 2trtog. Fasten off.
With RS facing, join B in a 2ch sp.
2nd round: [3ch, 2dtrtog, 2ch, 3dtrtog] in same 2ch sp as join, 4ch, * [3dtrtog, 2ch, 3dtrtog] in next 2ch sp, 4ch, rep from * 4 more times, ss in 2dtrtog. Fasten off.
With RS facing, join E in a 4ch sp.
3rd round: [2ch, 3trtog, 4ch, 4trtog] in same 4ch sp as join, * 2ch, 4trtog in next 2ch sp, 2ch, [4trtog, 4ch, 4trtog] in next 4ch sp, rep from * 4 more times, 2ch, 4trtog in last 2ch sp, 2ch, ss in 3trtog. Fasten off.

throw
Make 9 more flower hexagons in the colour combination given. Make 8 using C for B and 20 using E for A and D for B.

to make up
Join hexagons
Lay out the hexagons with points to top and lower edge to form the design by placing 4 white flowers in the centre, then surround them with a ring of 10 lilac flowers, then a ring of 16 white flowers, then two pink flowers at each corner.
Keeping flowers in order given, join short edges along each line of flowers, then join lines of flowers.

Joining row

With RS of hexagons together, line up the spaces, join in corner sps and work 3dc in these two 4ch sps together, 3dc in each of next two 2ch sps together and 3dc in corner 4ch sps together, for short joins fasten off, for lines of hexagons, continue matching and joining sps to end, then fasten off.

Darn in ends. Press lightly on WS.

make a bigger throw

For a throw that's about 100 x 104cm (39½ x 41in) you'll need approximately 1 more 50g ball in A, 2 in C and 3 in E. Make another 14 motifs using A, C and E to complete the ring of flowers in pink, and 12 motifs using D and E to fill in the corners.

charted version of flower hexagon

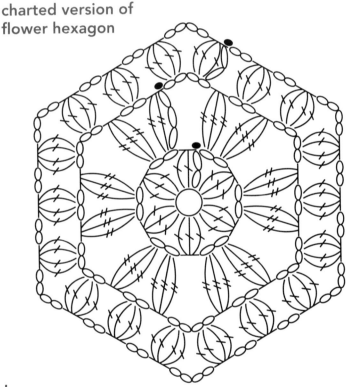

key

○   **ch** = chain

●   **ss** = slip stitch

+   **dc** = double crochet

T   **tr** = treble

   2trtog = leaving last loop of each st on hook, work 2tr, yrh and pull through 3 loops on hook

   3trtog = leaving last loop of each st on hook, work 3tr, yrh and pull through 4 loops on hook

   4trtog = leaving last loop of each st on hook, work 4tr, yrh and pull through 5 loops on hook

   2dtrtog = leaving last loop of each st on hook, work 2dtr, yrh and pull through 3 loops on hook

3dtrtog = leaving last loop of each st on hook, work 3dtr, yrh and pull through 4 loops on hook

wild flower *throw*

Stylised flowers, each made from four simple triangles in shades of pink and red, are set into lacy, soft green squares for this modern crochet version of an appliqué patchwork throw. It would be just perfect for a conservatory or garden room.

SIZE
111 x 111cm (43¾ x 43¾in)

YOU WILL NEED
Approximately:
180g of pure wool or wool rich DK yarn in shades of pink and red (A)
15g same in dark green (B)
10 x 50g balls same in pale green (C)
3.50mm (US E/4) crochet hook

TENSION
Triangles measure 11cm (4¼in) along each edge, each square measures 33 x 33cm (13 x 13in), when pressed, using 3.50mm (US E/4) hook. Change hook size, if necessary, to obtain this size triangle and square.

ABBREVIATIONS
ch = chain; **cont** = continue; **dc** = double crochet; **dtr** = double treble; **foll** = following; **rep** = repeat; **RS** = right side; **sp** = space; **ss** = slip stitch; **st(s)** = stitch(es); **tr** = treble; **WS** = wrong side; **[ ]** = work instructions in square brackets as directed.

NOTES
• Use as many different shades of pink and red as you can find. You'll need about 5g in any one shade to work a triangle.
• When changing colours on the 2nd round of the edging, always pull through the last loop of the last stitch in a colour with the next colour.

petals
Using A, wind yarn around finger to form a ring.
1st round (RS): 1ch, 1dc in ring, [3ch, 3dc in ring] twice, 3ch, 2dc in ring, ss in first dc.
2nd round: Ss in first 3ch sp, 1ch, [1dc, 6ch, 1tr] in same 3ch sp, [1tr in each of next 3dc, 1tr in next 3ch sp, 4ch, 1tr in same 3ch sp] twice, 1tr in each of next 3dc, ss in 2nd ch.
3rd round: Ss in first 4ch sp, 1ch, [1dc, 6ch, 2tr] in same 4ch sp, [1tr in each of next 5tr, 2tr in next 4ch sp, 4ch, 2tr in same 4ch sp] twice, 1tr in each of next 5tr, 1tr in first 4ch sp, ss in 2nd ch.
4th round: Ss in first 4ch sp, 1ch, [1dc, 6ch, 2tr] in same 4ch sp, [1tr in each of next 9tr, 2tr in next 4ch sp, 4ch, 2tr in same 4ch sp] twice, 1tr in each of next 9tr, 1tr in first 4ch sp, ss in 2nd ch.
Fasten off.
Using different shades of A, make 36 petals.

square
With RS facing, arrange 4 petals of varying shades with ends of rounds in the centre to form a flower. Using B, wind yarn around finger to form a ring.
Centre round: 1ch, 1dc in ring, 3dc in 4ch sp of first petal, [1dc in ring, 3dc in 4ch sp of next petal] 3 times, ss in first dc.
Fasten off.

edging

With RS facing, join C in 4ch sp at top right of one of the petals.

1st round: 1ch, * [1dc, 3ch, 1dc] in 4ch sp, [3ch, miss next tr, 1dc in foll tr] 6 times along top of petal, 3ch, [1dc, 3ch, 1dc] in next 4ch sp, [3ch, miss next tr, 1dc in foll tr] 5 times down side of petal, 3ch, miss next tr, ss in foll tr, ss in corresponding tr of next petal, [3ch, miss 1tr, 1dc in foll tr] 5 times up side of next petal, 3ch, rep from * 3 more times, ss in first dc.

2nd round: Ss in corner 3ch sp, 1ch, * [1dc, 3ch, 1dc] in corner 3ch sp, [3ch, 1dc in next 3ch sp] 7 times, 3ch, [1dc, 3ch, 1dc] in next corner 3ch sp, [3ch, 1dc in next 3ch sp] 4 times, 3ch, ss in foll 3ch sp of this petal, ss in corresponding 3ch sp of next petal, [3ch, 1dc in next 3ch sp] 4 times, 3ch, rep from * 3 more times, ss in first dc.

3rd round: Ss in corner 3ch sp, 1ch, * [1dc, 3ch, 1dc] in corner 3ch sp, [3ch, 1dc in next 3ch sp] 4 times, 5ch, [1dc in next 3ch sp, 3ch] 4 times, [1dc, 3ch, 1dc] in corner 3ch sp, [3ch, 1dc in next 3ch sp] 3 times, 3ch, ss in next 3ch sp, ss in corresponding 3ch sp of next petal, [3ch, 1dc in next 3ch sp] 3 times, 3ch, rep from * 3 more times, ss in first dc.

4th round: Ss in corner 3ch sp, 1ch, * [1dc, 3ch, 1dc] in corner 3ch sp, [3ch, 1dc in next 3ch sp] 4 times, 1ch, [1tr in 5ch sp, 1ch] 6 times, [1dc in next 3ch sp, 3ch] 4 times, [1dc, 3ch, 1dc] in corner 3ch sp, [3ch, 1dc in next 3ch sp] twice, 3ch, ss in foll 3ch sp, ss in corresponding 3ch sp of next petal, [3ch, 1dc in next 3ch sp] twice, 3ch, rep from * 3 more times, ss in first dc.

5th round: Ss in corner 3ch sp, 1ch, * [1dc, 3ch, 1dc] in corner 3ch sp, [3ch, 1dc in next 3ch sp] 4 times, 1ch, [1tr in next 1ch sp, 1ch] 3 times, [1tr, 3ch, 1tr] in foll 1ch sp, [1ch, 1tr in next 1ch sp] 3 times, 1ch, [1dc in next 3ch sp, 3ch] 4 times, [1dc, 3ch, 1dc] in corner 3ch sp, 3ch, 1dc in next 3ch sp, 3ch, ss in foll 3ch sp, ss in corresponding 3ch sp of next petal, 3ch, 1dc in next 3ch sp, 3ch, rep from * 3 more times, ss in first dc.

6th round: Ss in corner 3ch sp, 1ch, * [1dc, 3ch, 1dc] in corner 3ch sp, [3ch, 1dc in next 3ch sp] 4 times, 1ch, [1tr in next 1ch sp, 1ch] 4 times, [1tr, 3ch, 1tr] in next 3ch sp, [1ch, 1tr in next 1ch sp] 4 times, 1ch, [1dc in next 3ch sp, 3ch] 4 times, [1dc, 3ch, 1dc] in corner 3ch sp, 3ch, ss in next 3ch sp, ss in corresponding 3ch sp of next petal, 3ch, rep from * 3 more times, ss in first dc.

7th round Ss in corner 3ch sp, 1ch, ss in same 3ch sp, * [3ch, 1dc in next 3ch sp] 4 times, 1ch, [1tr in next 1ch sp, 1ch] 5 times, [1tr, 3ch, 1tr] in next 3ch sp, 1ch, [1tr in next 1ch sp, 1ch] 5 times, [1dc in next 3ch sp, 3ch] 4 times **, ss in each of next 2 corner 3ch sps, rep from * 2 more times, then rep from * to **, ss in last corner 3ch sp, ss in 2nd ss.

8th round: Ss in first 3ch sp, [1ch, 1dc] in same 3ch sp, 2ch, * [1tr in next dc, 1tr in next 3ch sp] 3 times, 1tr in next dc, [1tr in next 1ch sp, 1tr in next tr] 6 times, [1tr, 3ch, 1tr] in next 3ch sp, [1tr in next tr, 1tr in next 1ch sp] 6 times, [1tr in next dc, 1tr in next 3ch sp] 4 times **, 1dtr between next 2 ss, 1tr in next 3ch sp, rep from * 2 more times, then rep from * to **, 1dtr between last 2 ss, ss in 2nd ch.

9th round: 1ch, 1dc in same place as ss, 2ch, * [1tr in each st] to next 3ch sp, [1tr, 3ch, 1tr] in 3ch sp, rep from * 3 more times, [1tr in each st] to start of round, ss in 2nd ch.
Fasten off.
Varying the colours for the petals, make 8 more squares.
Press squares lightly on WS.

join squares

Arrange squares in 3 rows of 3 squares. With RS facing, join yarn in corner 3ch sp of first square, with WS tog, join first 2 squares.

Joining row: 1ch, 1dc in same sp as join, * 3ch, 1dc in corner 3ch sp of 2nd square, [3ch, miss next tr of first square, 1dc in foll tr, 3ch, miss next tr of 2nd square, 1dc in foll tr] 22 times, 3ch, 1dc in corner 3ch sp of first square, 3ch, 1dc in corner 3ch sp of 2nd

square, 3ch, line up 3rd and 4th squares, 1dc in corner 3ch sp of 3rd square, rep from * to join 3rd and 4th squares, then join 5th and 6th squares, ending 1dc in corner 3ch sp of 6th square. Fasten off.

Working in the same way join 3rd line of squares to 2nd line of squares, then join across in the other direction.

edging

With RS facing, join C in lower right corner 3ch sp.

1st round: 1ch, * [1dc, 3ch, 1dc] in corner 3ch sp, ** [3ch, miss 1tr, 1dc in next tr] 22 times ***, [3ch, 1dc in next sp] 3 times, rep from ** once more, then rep from ** to ***, 3ch, rep from * 3 more times, ss in first dc.

2nd round: Using C, ss in corner 3ch sp, 1ch, [1dc, 5ch, 1tr] in same 3ch sp, * [using A and changing shade as wished, 3tr in next 3ch sp, using C, 1tr in foll 3ch sp] 36 times, using A, 3tr in next 3ch sp **, [using C, 1tr, 3ch, 1tr] in corner 3ch sp, rep from * two more times, then rep from * to **, using C, ss in 2nd ch. Cont in C.

3rd round: Ss in corner 3ch sp, 1ch, [1dc, 3ch, 1dc] in same 3ch sp, * 1dc in next tr, [4ch, 1dc in next tr in C] 37 times **, [1dc, 3ch, 1dc] in corner 3ch sp, rep from * 2 more times, then rep from * to **, ss in first dc.

4th round: Ss in corner 3ch sp, 1ch, [1dc, 5ch, 1tr] in same 3ch sp, * 1tr in each of next 2dc, [3tr in 4ch sp, 1tr in next dc] 37 times, 1tr in foll dc **, [1tr, 3ch, 1tr] in corner 3ch sp, rep from * two more times, then rep from * to **, ss in 2nd ch, turn.

5th round: 1ch, 1dc in same place as ss, * [1dc in each tr] to corner, 4dc in 3ch sp, rep from * 3 more times, ss in first dc. Fasten off.

Press lightly on WS. Darn in ends.

make a bigger throw or a cushion

For a bigger throw

For a throw that measures 111 x 146cm (43¾ x 57½in), you'll need approximately 60g extra in A, 5g extra in B and 4 x 50g balls extra in C.

Make 12 more petals and turn them into 3 more squares. Assemble and work edging in the same way as given, repeating instructions as necessary along the side edges.

For a cushion

For a cushion front that measures 41 x 41cm (16 x 16in), you'll need just 20g in shades of A, 5g in B and 2 x 50g balls in C. Work 4 petals and one square as given, then adjusting the repeats to fit, work edging.

roses & daisies *throw*

Use even the tiniest scraps from your yarn stash to make this stunning coverlet. There are two flower shapes to play with, a rose with raised popcorns at the centre and a flat daisy-like bloom. Each flower uses three different colours and the aim is to make each combination different to give a really wild flower design.

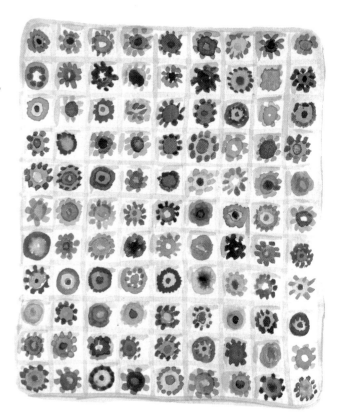

SIZE
83 x 101cm (32¾ x 39¾in)

YOU WILL NEED
Approximately 400g of wool, wool-mix, cotton and cotton-mix DK yarn in as many shades as possible of pink, fuchsia, red, maroon, purple, blue, green, lime, olive, turquoise, gold and orange
8 x 50g balls of wool-mix DK in cream (A)
2.50mm (US C/2) and 3.50mm (US E/4) crochet hooks

TENSION
Each motif, when edged, measures 9 x 9cm (3½ x 3½in), using 3.50mm (US E/4) hook. Change hook size, if necessary, to obtain this size square.

ABBREVIATIONS
ch = chain; **cont** = continue; **dc** = double crochet; **dtr** = double treble; **foll** = following; **htr** = half treble; **rep** = repeat; **RS** = right side; **sp(s)** = space(s); **ss** = slip stitch; **st(s)** = stitch(es); **tr** = treble; **2trtog** = leaving last loop of each tr on hook, work 2tr, yrh and pull through 3 loops on hook; **3trtog** = leaving last loop of each tr on hook, work 3tr, yrh and pull through 4 loops on hook; **WS** = wrong side; **yrh** = yarn around hook; **[ ]** = work instructions in square brackets as directed.

NOTES
• **For the rose squares** use shades of pink, fuchsia, red, lilac, purple, lime, pale green, olive, blue green and mid green.
• **For the daisy squares** use shades of blue, lilac, purple, orange, gold, lime, olive, bright green, pale green and turquoise.

rose square
Using 3.50mm (US E/4) hook and first colour make 5ch, ss in first ch to form a ring.
1st round (RS): 1ch, 8dc in ring, ss in first dc. 8 sts.
2nd round: 1ch, 2dc in same place as ss, 2dc in each of next 7dc, change to 2nd colour, ss in first dc.
Cont in 2nd colour.
3rd round: [3ch, 3tr in next dc, remove hook, insert in top of first tr, catch loop and pull through, 3ch, 1dc in foll dc] 8 times omitting last dc, change to 3rd colour, ss in first dc.
Cont in 3rd colour.
4th round: 4ch, 3dtr in same place as ss, [1ch, 4dtr in next dc] 7 times, 1ch, ss in 4th ch. Fasten off.
Join A in a 1ch sp.
5th round: 4ch, 1tr in same sp as join, * 4ch, 2dc in next 1ch sp, 4ch, [1tr, 1ch, 1tr] in foll 1ch sp, rep from * two more times, 4ch, 2dc in next 1ch sp, 4ch, ss in 3rd ch.
6th round: 2ch, * [1tr, 1ch, 1tr] in next 1ch sp, 1htr in next tr, 4dc in next 4ch sp, 1dc in each of next 2dc, 4dc in foll 4ch sp, 1htr in next tr, rep from * 3 more times omitting last htr, ss in 2nd ch. Fasten off.
Using a different combination for 1st, 2nd and 3rd colours each time, if possible but always using A for 5th and 6th rounds, make 49 rose squares.

daisy square

Using 3.50mm (US E/4) hook and first colour, make 6ch, ss in first ch to form a ring.

1st round (RS): 1ch, 12dc in ring, change to 2nd colour, ss in first dc, 12 sts.

Cont in 2nd colour.

2nd round: 4ch, 1dtr in same place as ss, 2dtr in each of next 11dc, ss in 4th ch. 24 sts.

Fasten off.

Join 3rd colour between two pairs of dtr.

3rd round: 2ch, 2trtog in same place as join, [3ch, 3trtog between next two pairs of dtr] 11 times, 3ch, ss in 2trtog. Fasten off.

Join A in a 3ch sp.

4th round: 1ch, 4dc in same 3ch sp, * [2tr, 1ch, 2tr] in foll 3ch sp, 4dc in each of next two 3ch sps, rep from * two more times, [2tr, 1ch, 2tr] in next 3ch sp, 4dc in last 3ch sp, ss in first dc.

5th round: 1ch, * 1dc in each of 4dc, 1dc in tr, 1htr in next tr, [1tr, 1ch, 1tr] in 1ch sp, 1htr in next tr, 1dc in foll tr, 1dc in each of next 4dc, rep from * 3 more times, ss in first dc. Fasten off.

Using a different combination for first, 2nd and 3rd colours each time, if possible but always using A for 4th and 5th rounds, make 50 daisy squares.

throw

Press squares lightly on WS avoiding raised stitches. Starting with a daisy square at each corner and alternating motifs, arrange

charted version of rose square

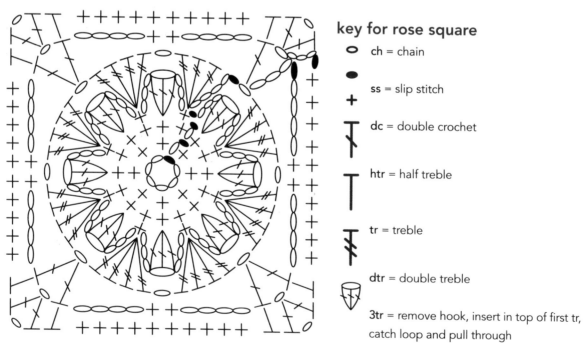

key for rose square

o   **ch** = chain

•   **ss** = slip stitch

+   **dc** = double crochet

T   **htr** = half treble

T   **tr** = treble

U   **dtr** = double treble

3tr = remove hook, insert in top of first tr, catch loop and pull through

squares in an oblong, 9 squares across by 11 squares down. Using 3.50mm (US E/4) hook, A and with RS together join first squares of 1st and 2nd lines of squares by working 1dc in both corner sps together, then 1dc in next st of both squares together to corner, 1dc in both corner sps together, 1ch, join each pair of squares for 1st and 2nd lines of squares in this way. Fasten off. Taking care not to twist the 1st line of squares when joining next line of squares, join all short lines of squares, then join all long lines of squares in the same way.

edging

Using 3.50mm (US E/4) hook and with RS facing, join A in a corner 1ch sp.

1st round: 1ch, 3dc in same sp as join, * 1dc in each of next 14 sts, placing first part tr in next 1ch sp and 2nd part tr in foll 1ch sp work 2trtog, rep from * to next corner omitting last 2trtog, 3dc in corner 1ch sp, rep from * along each side omitting last 2trtog and 3dc, ss in first dc.

Change to 2.50mm (US C/2) hook and work 1 round of crab st (dc backwards) ending ss in first dc.

Fasten off.

to make up

Darn in ends. Press seams and edging.

key for daisy square

○ ch = chain

● ss = slip stitch

— dc = double crochet

T htr = half treble

T̅ tr = treble

T̿ dtr = double treble

 2trtog = leaving last loop of each tr on hook, work 2tr, yrh and pull through 3 loops on hook

  3trtog = leaving last loop of each tr on hook, work 3tr, yrh and pull through 4 loops on hook

charted version of daisy square

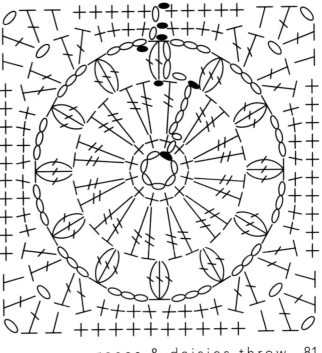

Width (for sand and sky) 65cm (25½in)
Length (excluding tassels) 86.5cm (34in)

YOU WILL NEED
Approximately:
75g alpaca DK in sand (A)
10g metallic 4ply in pale gold (B)
25g pure wool DK in dark sand (C)
10g mohair 4ply in pale sand (D)
15g mohair DK in white (E)
20g metallic 4ply in silver (F)
15g pure wool DK in pale sea green (G)
10g metallic 4ply in turquoise (H)
20g silk DK in pale turquoise (I)
10g mohair 2ply in deep sea green (J)
10g wool mix 4ply in shaded grey blue (K)
20g wool mix DK in mid sea green (L)
40g silk DK in shaded bright blue (M)
10g pure wool DK in bright sea green (N)
20g alpaca mix DK in sky blue (O)
10g mohair DK in cloud grey (P)
40g pure wool DK in pale sky blue (Q)
4.00mm (US F/5) crochet hook

TENSION
Each shell measures 9 x 8cm (3½ x 3⅛in), five 2tr
groups and 6 rows measure 11cm (4¼in) over
sand patt, one chevron and 3 rows measure
5cm (2in) over sea patt, three 3trtog and 3ch
groups and 4 rows measure 7cm (2¾in) over sky
patt, all using 4.00mm (US F/5) hook. Change
hook size, if necessary, to obtain these sizes.

ABBREVIATIONS
ch = chain; **cont** = continue; **dc** = double crochet;
2dctog = [insert hook in next st, yrh and pull loop
through] twice, yrh and pull through 3 loops on
hook; **dtr** = double treble; **2dtrtog** = leaving last
loop of each dtr on hook, work 2dtr, yrh and pull
through 3 loops on hook; **foll** = following;
patt = pattern; **rep** = repeat; **RS** = right side;
sp = space; **ss** = slip stitch; **st(s)** = stitch(es);
tr = treble; **2trtog** = leaving last loop of each tr
on hook, work 2tr, yrh and pull through 3 loops
on hook; **3trtog** = leaving last loop of each tr on
hook, work 3tr, yrh and pull through 4 loops on
hook; **4trtog** = leaving last loop of each tr on
hook, work 4tr, yrh and pull through 5 loops on
hook; **trtr** = triple treble; **WS** = wrong side;
yrh = yarn around hook; **[ ]** = work instructions in
square brackets as directed.

NOTES
• Yarn amounts are based on yarns used in the
original. Tensions may vary with weight of yarns.
• The fabric for the sea is wider than the sand
and sky so it flutes and adds to the wavy effect.
• Yarn changes are given, but you can simply
plan colour groups and work yarns at random.

seascape
wall hanging

*Simple texture stitch patterns in an amazing mix of different
colour and texture yarns give an impression of sand, sea and
sky. Hang the finished crochet picture on your wall or use it as
an unusual throw or comforter. This really is one for which you
can dive into your stash and
fish out all those unusual
and glamorous yarns you
couldn't resist but thought
you'd never find a use for.
Be inspired by the yarns
listed or go freestyle with
your own colour theme.*

shells and sand
Using A, make 17ch.
1st row (RS): 1dc in 6th ch from
hook, [27ch, 1dc in 6th ch from
hook] 6 times, 12ch, turn.
2nd row: 1dc in 2nd ch from
hook, [6dtr in next 6ch sp, 11ch]
6 times, 6dtr in last 6ch sp, 1dc in end ch.
3rd row: 5ch, * [1dtr, 1ch] in each of next 6dtr, 1dc in 11ch sp, 1ch,
rep from * 5 more times, [1dtr, 1ch] in each of last 6dtr, 1trtr in last dc.
4th row: [4ch, 4trtog in next sp] to end, 1dtr in 5th ch.
5th row: Ss between dtr and first 4trtog, 7ch, * [1dc, 4ch, 1dc] in
each of next six 4ch sps, 1dc in foll 4ch sp, rep from * 5 more times,
[1dc, 4ch, 1dc] in each of last six 4ch sps, 2ch, 1dtr in 4ch sp.
Fasten off.
Join B in 2ch sp.
6th row: 5ch, [3dc in next 4ch sp, 2ch] to end omitting last ch,
1dtr in 7ch sp.
Fasten off.
Join C in 1ch sp.
7th row: 1ch, 1dc in same sp as join, [3ch, 1dc in next 2ch sp] to
end, 3ch, 1dc in 5ch sp.
8th row: Ss in first 3ch sp, 1ch, 1dc in same sp, 2ch, * [2tr, 3ch, 2tr]
in each of next four 3ch sps **, placing one part tr in each of next
2 sps work 2trtog, rep from * 5 more times, then rep from * to **,

1ch, 1tr in last 3ch sp.
Fasten off.
Join D in 1ch sp.
9th row: 1ch, 1dc in same sp as join, 2ch, [2tr, 3ch, 2tr] in each 3ch sp, 1tr in 2ch sp.
9th row forms the sand patt.
Cont in patt, work 9 more rows fastening off and joining colours in order A, B, D, C, A, B, C, D, A.
Join B in end 2tr of last row.
19th row: 1ch, 1dc in same sp as join, 5ch, [1dc in next 3ch sp, 4ch] 27 times, 1dc in last 3ch sp, 2ch, 1tr in 2ch sp.
Fasten off.

sea

Join E in tr.
1st row (WS): 1ch, 1dc in tr, [4ch, 1dc in next 4ch sp, 6ch, ss in previous dc, 4ch, 1dc in foll 4ch sp] 14 times, placing last dc in end sp.
2nd row: 1ch, 1dc in first dc, * 1ch, [1dtr, 1ch] 6 times in next 6ch sp, 1dc in next dc, rep from * 13 more times.
Fasten off.
Join F in first 1ch sp.
3rd row: 1ch, 1dc in same sp as join, * 2dc in each of next 2sps, [2dc, 2ch, 2dc] in foll sp, 2dc in each of next 2sps, 1dc in each of foll 2 sps, rep from * to end omitting last dc.
Fasten off.
Join G in 2nd dc.
4th row: 1dc in same place as join, 2ch, 1tr in next dc, * 1tr in each of foll 4dc, [1tr, 2ch, 1tr] in 2ch sp, 1tr in each of next 4dc, 2trtog, miss 2dc, 2trtog, rep from * to end omitting last 2trtog and missing last dc.
Fasten off.
Join H in 2trtog.
5th row: 1ch, 1dc in next tr, * 1dc in each of foll 4 sts, [1dc, 2ch, 1dc] in 2ch sp, 1dc in each of next 4 sts, [2dctog] twice, rep from * to end omitting last 2dctog.
Fasten off.
Join I in 2dctog.
6th row: 2ch, 1tr in next dc, * 1tr in each of next 4 sts, [1tr, 2ch, 1tr] in 2ch sp, 1tr in each of next 4 sts, [2trtog] twice, rep from * to end omitting last 2trtog.
5th and 6th rows form dc and tr chevron sea patt.
Patt 1 row G and 1 row F.
Work 6th row only for tr chevron sea patt.
Cont in patt work 16 more rows in colour order E, I, H, J, I, K, J, F, L, J, M, N, K, M, L and M. Do not fasten off after last row.
Cont in M.

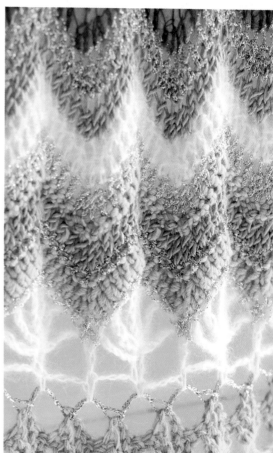

horizon

1st row: 1ch, 1dc in first st, 2ch, 1dtr in next tr, 2trtog, 2dctog, [1dc, 2ch, 1dc] in 2ch sp, * 2dctog, 2trtog, [2dtrtog] twice, 2trtog, 2dctog, [1dc, 2ch, 1dc] in 2ch sp, rep from * 12 more times, 2dctog, 2trtog, 2dtrtog.

2nd row: 1ch, 1dc in first 2dtrtog, 7ch, [1dc in next 2ch sp, 4ch, 1tr between next pair of 2dtrtog, 4ch] 13 times, 1dc in last 2ch sp, 4ch, 1tr in last dtr.

3rd row: 1ch, 1dc in first tr, [3dc in next 4ch sp, 1dc in next st] to end, placing last dc in 3rd ch.

Fasten off.

sky

Join O in first dc.

1st row: 1ch, 1dc in same place as join, 3ch, [miss next 3dc, 1tr in foll dc, 3ch, 3trtog over previous tr, 1ch] 27 times, miss next 3dc, 1tr in last dc.

2nd row: 1ch, 1dc in first tr, 2ch, miss first 1ch sp, [1tr in next 1ch sp, 3ch, 3trtog over previous tr, 1ch] 26 times, 1tr in 2nd ch.

3rd row: 1ch, 1dc in first tr, 2ch, [1tr in next 1ch sp, 3ch, 3trtog over previous tr, 1ch] 27 times working last rep in end ch sp, 1tr in 2nd ch.

Fasten off.

Using P, work 2nd row again. Using E, work 3rd and 2nd rows again. Using Q, work 3rd row again.

Next row: 1ch, 1dc in first tr, 2ch, 3tr in each 3ch sp, 1tr in last tr. 83 sts.

Cont in Q, work 6 rows tr.

Fasten off.

edging

With RS facing, join A at lower right and changing colours for each section, work 1 row of dc evenly up right edge, along top and down left edge.

to make up

Press, taking care over different yarn fibres. Darn in ends. Using A, make 7 tassels, approximately 14cm (5½in) long and sew one tassel on the base of each shell.

make a bigger picture

It's easy to make the picture longer, just carry on working in the different stitch patterns until the sand, the sea and the sky are the length you want. If you want to make the picture wider, work an extra shell for each 9cm (3½in) added to the width. The other stitch patterns relate to the shells so just work more repeats.

SIZES

Blanket 44 x 56cm (17¼ x 22in)
Sheep height approximately 15cm (6in)

YOU WILL NEED

FOR THE BLANKET
Approximately:
25g of pure wool or wool mix DK yarn in
meadow green (A)
15g same in each of bright grass green (B),
pale grass green (C) and clover (D)
10g same in each of corn yellow (E),
mustard yellow (F) and forest green (G)
30g same in sky blue (H)
100g same in hedgerow green (I)
4.00mm (US F/5) crochet hook

FOR THE SHEEP
50g of pure wool DK in cream
Pink and black embroidery wool
Washable polyester stuffing
2 small buttons
3.50mm (US E/4) crochet hook

TENSION

Each first line field measures 11 x 12cm (4¼ x
4¾in), each 2nd line field measures 8.5 x 8cm (3⅜
x 3⅛in), each 3rd line field measures 6.5 x 6.5cm
(2½ x 2½in), each 4th line field measures 5 x 5cm
(2 x 2in), 10 dc and 1ch sps and 11 rows to 5cm
(2in) over sky patt, all using 4.00mm (US F/5)
hook. Change hook size, if necessary, to obtain
these size squares and this tension.

ABBREVIATIONS

ch = chain; **dc** = double crochet; **2dctog** = [insert
hook in next st, yrh and pull loop through] twice,
yrh and pull through 3 loops on hook; **3dctog** =
[insert hook in next st, yrh and pull loop through]
3 times, yrh and pull through 3 loops on hook;
foll = following; **htr** = half treble; **patt** = pattern;
rep = repeat; **RS** = right side; **sp(s)** = space(s);
ss = slip stitch; **st(s)** = stitch(es); **yrh** = yarn around
hook; **WS** = wrong side; **[ ]** = work instructions in
square brackets as directed.

NOTES

• Yarn amounts for different colours are given as
a guide but you can use any colour or a different
texture yarn as long as it works to a DK weight.
• The fields are simple blocks of double crochet
with spaces along each side for easy joining.
• When working the joins, always check back that
you haven't missed a space before fastening off.
• If you get the correct size field blocks, then your
tension for the sheep should be correct on the
smaller hook. If you need to change hook size for
the fields, change to the corresponding hook size
for the sheep.
• If the sheep is for a baby, embroider the eyes.

landscape
play blanket

*Here's a really simple patchwork blanket, all in double crochet
apart from a few fully explained multiple stitches, with the colours
and shapes arranged to
look like a child's
drawing of fields, hills
and sky. As an irresistible
extra, there's a little sheep
toy to play with too.*

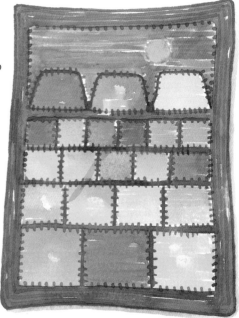

fields

1st line of fields

Using A, make 22ch.

1st row (RS): Working into strand at back of each ch, 1dc in 2nd
ch from hook, [1ch, miss 1ch, 1dc in next ch] to end.

2nd row: 1ch, 1dc in first dc, 1ch, 1dc in next dc, [1dc in next 1ch
sp, 1dc in foll dc] to last 1ch sp, 1ch, miss 1ch sp, 1dc in last dc.

3rd row: 1ch, 1dc in first dc, 1ch, miss first 1ch sp, 1dc in each dc
to last 1ch sp, 1ch, miss 1ch sp, 1dc in last dc.

3rd row forms patt. There are 17dc at centre with sps at each end.
Patt 15 more rows.

Last row: 1ch, 1dc in first dc, 1ch, miss 1ch sp, 1dc in next dc,
[1ch, miss next dc, 1dc in foll dc] to last 1ch sp, 1ch, miss 1ch sp,
1dc in last dc.
Fasten off.
Make one more first line field in each of B and C.

Join 1st line of fields

With RS facing, join I in 1ch sp at lower right corner of field in A.
With WS together, hold field in B behind.

Joining row (RS): 1ch, 1dc in same place as join, 1ch, 1dc in
corresponding corner sp of field in B, [1ch, miss next sp in A, 1dc

in foll sp in A, 1ch, miss next sp in B, 1dc in foll sp in B] to end.
Fasten off.
Join B and C fields in the same way.

2nd line of fields
Using A, make 16ch.
Work first, 2nd and 3rd rows as given for first line of fields.
After 3rd row, there are 11dc at centre with sps at each end.
Patt 9 more rows, then work last row.
Fasten off.
Make one more 2nd line field in each of C, D and E.
Join 2nd line of fields
Using I and working in same way as joining first line of fields, join E to
C, C to D and D to A.

3rd line of fields
Using A, make 12ch.
Work first, 2nd and 3rd rows as given for first line of fields.
After 3rd row, there are 7dc at centre with sps at each end.
Patt 5 more rows, then work last row.
Fasten off.
Make one more 3rd line field in each of B, C, E and F.
Join 3rd line of fields
Using I and working in same way as joining first line of fields, join C
to A, A to F, F to E and E to B.

4th line of fields
Using A, make 10ch.
Work first, 2nd and 3rd rows as given for first line of fields.
After 3rd row, there are 5dc at centre with sps at each end.
Patt 3 more rows, then work last row.
Fasten off.
Make two more 4th line fields in B and one more in each of C, D
and E.
Join 4th line of fields
Using I and working in same way as joining first line of fields, join B
to D, D to E, E to B, B to C and C to A.

join lines of fields
Using I and working in the same way as before, with 1dc and 1ch in
each vertical join, join first, 2nd, 3rd and 4th lines of fields, noting
that 3rd line of fields has one space less, so joins should start and
end on 2nd and on 4th lines of fields.
Top edging row: With RS facing, join I in dc at right of 4th line of
fields, 1ch, 1dc in same place as join, 1dc in next 1ch sp, [1ch, 1dc in
next sp] to end, 1dc in last dc.
Fasten off.

hills

1st hill

Using A make 2ch.

1st row (RS): 3dc in 2nd ch from hook. 3 sts.

2nd row: 1ch, 2dc in each dc. 6 sts.

3rd row: 1ch, 2dc in first dc, [1dc in next dc, 2dc in foll dc] twice, 1dc in last dc. 9 sts.

4th row: 1ch, 2dc in first dc, [1dc in each of next 2dc, 2dc in foll dc] twice, 1dc in each of last 2dc. 12 sts.

5th row: 1ch, 2dc in first dc, [1dc in each of next 3dc, 2dc in foll dc] twice, 1dc in each of last 3dc. 15 sts.

6th row: 1ch, 2dc in first dc, [1dc in each of next 4dc, 2dc in foll dc] twice, 1dc in each of last 4dc. 18 sts.

7th row: 1ch, 2dc in first dc, [1dc in each of next 5dc, 2dc in foll dc] twice, 1dc in each of last 5dc. 21 sts.

8th row: 1ch, 2dc in first dc, [1dc in each of next 6dc, 2dc in foll dc] twice, 1dc in each of last 6dc. 24 sts.

9th row: 1ch, 2dc in first dc, [1dc in each of next 7dc, 2dc in foll dc] twice, 1dc in each of last 7dc. 27 sts.

10th row: 1ch, 2dc in first dc, [1dc in each of next 8dc, 2dc in foll dc] twice, 1dc in each of last 8dc. 30 sts.

Fasten off.

Make one more hill in each of D and G.

join hills and fields

With RS facing hold hill in G upside down and join I in first row-end, have hills in A and D ready.

Lower edging row (RS): 1ch, 1dc in same place as join, * [1ch, miss 1 row-end, 1dc in next row-end] 4 times, 1ch, 1dc in centre ch, [1ch, miss 1 row-end, 1dc in next row-end] 5 times across edge of hill in G, 1ch, 1dc in first row-end of hill in A, rep from * across edge of hill in A, 1ch, 1dc in first row-end of hill in D, rep from * across edge of hill in D.

With WS together and top edging row level with last row, hold fields behind hills. Starting and ending with a dc in a lower edging row sp, join hills and fields in same way as joining fields.

sky

With RS facing, join I in first dc at right of hill in D.

Edging row (RS): 1ch, 1dc in same place as join, [1ch, 1dc in next dc] 27 times, * insert hook in next dc and pull loop through, yrh, insert hook in foll dc, yrh and pull loop through, yrh and pull through first 2 loops on hook, [yrh, insert hook in next sp, yrh and pull loop through, yrh and pull through first 2 loops on hook] twice, yrh, insert hook in first dc of next hill, yrh and pull loop through, yrh and pull through first 2 loops on hook, insert hook in next dc, yrh and pull loop through, yrh and pull through all 7 loops on hook **, [1ch, 1dc in next dc] 26 times, rep from * to **, [1ch, 1dc in next dc] 28 times.

Fasten off.

With WS facing, join H in 4th 1ch sp of previous row.

1st row (WS): 1ch, 1dc in same place as join, [1ch, 1dc in next 1ch sp] 21 times, 1ch, work into next 6 sps as given from * to ** of edging row, [1ch, 1dc in next 1ch sp] 21 times, 1ch, work into next 6 sps as given from * to ** of edging row, [1ch, 1dc in next 1ch sp] 22 times, turn and leave last 3 sps.

2nd row: 1ch, miss first 1ch sp, ss in next 1ch sp, 1ch, 1dc in foll 1ch sp, *** [1ch, 1dc in next 1ch sp] 16 times, 1ch, work into next 6 sps as given from * to ** of edging row, rep from *** once more, [1ch, 1dc in next 1ch sp] 16 times, 1ch, ss in foll 1ch sp, turn.

3rd row: 1ch, miss first 1ch sp, ss in next 1ch sp, [1ch, 1dc in next 1ch sp] 12 times, 1ch, work into next 6 sps as given from * to ** of edging row, [1ch, 1dc in next 1ch sp] 11 times, 1ch, work into next 6 sps as given from * to ** of edging row, [1ch, 1dc in next 1ch sp] 12 times, 1ch, ss in next 1ch sp, turn.

4th row: 1ch, miss first 1ch sp, ss in next 1ch sp, 2ch, [1dc in next 1ch sp, 1ch] 9 times, 1dc in foll 1ch sp, *1ch, 1htr in next 1ch sp, 1ch, 1htr in next st, 1ch, 1htr in foll sp *, [1ch, 1dc in next 1ch sp] 10 times, rep from * to *, [1ch, 1dc in next 1ch sp] 10 times, 1ch, 1htr in foll 1ch sp, turn.

5th row: 1ch, 1dc in first 1ch sp, [1ch, 1dc in next 1ch sp] 36 times, turn.

6th row: 1dc in first 1ch sp, [1ch, 1dc in next 1ch sp] 35 times.

7th row: 1ch, 1dc in first dc, 1dc in first 1ch sp, [1ch, 1dc in next 1ch sp] 34 times, 1dc in last dc.

8th row: 1ch, 1dc in first dc, [1ch, 1dc in next 1ch sp] 34 times, 1ch, 1dc in last dc. 7th and 8th rows form the sky patt. Patt 9 more rows.

Fasten off.

sun

Using E, wind yarn around finger to form a ring.

1st round: 1ch, 6dc in ring, ss in first dc. 6 sts.

2nd round: 1ch, 2dc in each dc, ss in first dc. 12 sts.

3rd round: 1ch, 2dc in first dc, [1dc in next dc, 2dc in foll dc] 5 times, 1dc in last dc, ss in first dc. 18 sts.

4th round: 1ch, 2dc in first dc, [1dc in each of next 2dc, 2dc in foll dc] 5 times, 1dc in each of last 2dc, ss in first dc. 24 sts.

Fasten off leaving a long end.

border

With RS facing, join I in lower right corner sp.

1st round (RS): 1ch, * [1dc, 3ch, 1dc] in corner sp, 1ch, spacing sts evenly and working dc into sps or joins as necessary, [1dc, 1ch] 44 times up right edge, [1dc, 3ch, 1dc] in corner sp, 1ch, [1dc, 1ch] 32 times along top edge, rep from * down left edge and along lower edge, ss in first dc, ss in 3ch sp, turn.

2nd round: 1ch, 1dc in 3ch sp, * 1dc in next dc, [1dc in next 1ch sp, 1dc in foll dc] to corner, [1dc, 3ch, 1dc] in corner 3ch sp, rep from * along each edge omitting last dc, ss in first dc, turn.

3rd round: Ss in 3ch sp, 1ch, * [1dc, 3ch, 1dc] in corner 3ch sp, 1dc in each dc to next corner, rep from * to end, ss in first dc, ss in 3ch sp, turn.

4th round: 1ch, 1dc in 3ch sp, * 1dc in each dc to corner, [1dc, 3ch, 1dc] in corner 3ch sp, rep from * to end omitting last dc, ss in first dc, turn.

3rd and 4th rounds form dc border. Turning each time, work 5 more rounds dc.

Fasten off.

to make up

Press on WS using a damp cloth if necessary to set the stitches. Darn in ends. With RS facing, slip stitch sun in place at top right of sky, then work decorative straight stitches around the sun.

sheep toy

Head

Leaving a long end, wind yarn around finger to form a ring.

1st round (RS): 1ch, 7dc in ring, ss in first dc. 7 sts **.

2nd round: 1ch, 2dc in each dc, ss in first dc. 14 sts.

3rd and 4th rounds: 1ch, 1dc in each dc, ss in first dc.

5th round: 1ch, 2dc in each dc, ss in first dc. 28 sts.

Cont in dc, work 9 more rounds.

Turn head inside out, secure end then bring end through to RS and turn head to RS. Take a pinch between the starting round and 4th round and stitch

to make a smiley mouth, fastening off end on WS.

1st dec round: 1ch, [1dc in each of next 2dc, 2dctog] 7 times, ss in first dc. 21 sts.

Work 1 round dc.

2nd dec round: 1ch, [1dc in next dc, 2dctog] 7 times, ss in first dc. 14 sts.

Work 1 round dc. Stuff head.

3rd dec round: 1ch, [2dctog] 7 times, ss in first dc. 7 sts. Leaving a long end, fasten off. Thread end through tops of sts, draw up and fasten off securely.

Body

Work as given for head until 2nd round has been completed. 14 sts.

Work 1 round dc.

4th round: 1ch, 2dc in each dc, ss in first dc. 28 sts.

Work 1 round dc.

6th round: 1ch, 2dc in first dc, [1dc in next dc, 2dc in foll dc] 13 times, 1dc in last dc, ss in first dc. 42 sts.

Work 15 rounds dc.

1st dec round: 1ch, 1dc in each of first 11dc, [2dctog] 10 times, 1dc in each of last 11dc, ss in first dc. 32 sts.

Work 3 rounds dc.

2nd dec round: 1ch, 1dc in each of first 8dc, [2dctog] 8 times, 1dc in each of last 8dc, ss in first dc. 24 sts.

Work 3 rounds dc.

3rd dec round: 1ch, [2dctog] 12 times, ss in first st. 12 sts.

Neck

Work 2 rounds dc.

Fasten off.

Stuff body. With decreases at front of body and folding front neck in, sew on head at a cute angle.

Front legs

Work as head to **. Work 15 rounds dc.

Fasten off. Stuff legs.

Back legs

Work as head to **. Work 7 rounds dc.

1st inc round: 1ch, 2dc in each dc, ss in first dc. 14 sts.

Work 3 rounds dc.

2nd inc round: 1ch, 1dc in each of first 4dc, 2dc in each of next 6dc, 1dc in each of last 4dc, ss in first dc. 20 sts.

Work 5 rounds dc.

1st dec round: 1ch, [2dctog] 10 times, ss in first dc. 10 sts.
Work 1 round dc. Stuff leg.
2nd dec round: 1ch, [2dctog] 5 times, ss in first st. 5 sts.
Leaving a long end, fasten off, thread end through tops of sts, draw up and secure.

Tail
Work as head to **. Work 5 rounds dc.
Fasten off.

Ears
Make 2ch.
1st row: 5dc in 2nd ch from hook. 5 sts.
Work 6 rows dc.

Dec row: 1ch, 2dctog, 1dc in next dc, 2dctog. 3 sts.
Work 1 row dc.
Next row: 1ch, 3dctog.
Fasten off.

Topknot
[Make 5ch, ss in 5th ch from hook] 9 times.
Fasten off.

to make up
Sew on front and back legs and tail. With points to centre top of head, sew on ears. Curl topknot and sew on top of head. Using cream, stitch to make hollows for eyes, catching through to mouth to shape face. Using black, sew on buttons for eyes and using pink, stitch mouth.

chapter 4 *around the world*

tartan *blanket*

This crochet version of the famous Scots tartan pattern uses simple stitches to create a fabric with bands of colours and a grid of holes to weave narrow stripes of contrast colours through. You can adapt the colour scheme to give the effect of your favourite plaid.

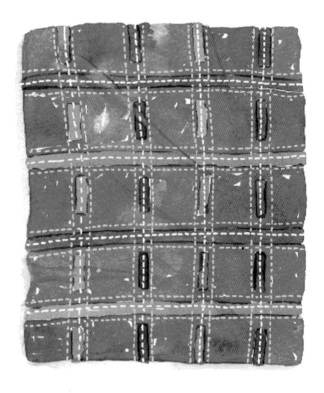

SIZE
76 x 90.5cm (30 x 35½in)

YOU WILL NEED
7 x 50g balls of Debbie Bliss Rialto DK in red (A)
2 x 50g balls same in each of navy (B) and green (C)
1 x 50g ball same in each of yellow (D) and cream (E)
4.00mm (US F/5) crochet hook

TENSION
18 sts and 12 rows to 10cm (4in) over tr and dc check patt, using 4.00mm (US F/5) hook. Change hook size, if necessary, to obtain this tension.

ABBREVIATIONS
ch = chain; **cont** = continue; **dc** = double crochet; **patt** = pattern; **RS** = right side; **sp(s)** = space(s); **ss** = slip stitch; **st(s)** = stitch(es); **tr** = treble; **[ ]** = work instructions in square brackets as directed.

NOTES
• When changing colours, always pull through the last loop of the last stitch in a colour block using the next colour.
• Count each chain space as a stitch.
• Use separate balls of yarn for each panel in B and C working over A yarn.
• If necessary, make the contrast chain lengths longer or shorter to fit the width and length of the blanket without puckering.

blanket
Using A, make 138ch.

1st row (RS): Cont in A, work into back strand of each ch, 1dc in 2nd ch from hook, 1dc in each of next 16ch, [1ch, miss 1ch, 1dc in each of foll 2ch, change to B, 1dc in each of next 3ch, 1ch, miss 1ch, 1dc in each of foll 3ch, change to A, 1dc in each of next 2ch, 1ch, miss 1ch, 1dc in each of foll 17ch, 1ch, miss 1ch, 1dc in each of next 2ch, change to C, 1dc in each of next 3ch, 1ch, miss 1ch, 1dc in each of foll 3ch, change to A, 1dc in each of next 2ch, 1ch, miss 1ch, 1dc in each of next 17ch] twice.

2nd row: Cont in A, 1dc in first dc, 2ch, 1tr in each of next 16dc, [1ch, miss 1ch, 1tr in each of foll 2dc, change to C, 1tr in each of next 3dc, 1ch, miss 1ch, 1tr in each of foll 3dc, change to A, 1tr in each of next 2dc, 1ch, miss 1ch, 1tr in each of foll 17dc, 1ch, miss 1ch, 1tr in each of next 2dc, change to B, 1tr in each of next 3dc, 1ch, miss 1ch, 1tr in each of foll 3dc, change to A, 1tr in each of next 2dc, 1ch, miss 1ch, 1tr in each of next 17dc] twice.

3rd row: Cont in A, 1ch, 1dc in each of first 17tr, [1ch, miss 1ch, 1dc in each of foll 2tr, change to B, 1dc in each of next 3tr, 1ch, miss 1ch, 1dc in each of foll 3tr, change to A, 1dc in each of next 2tr, 1ch, miss 1ch, 1dc in each of foll 17tr, 1ch, miss 1ch, 1dc in

each of next 2tr, change to C, 1dc in each of next 3tr, 1ch, miss 1ch, 1dc in each of foll 3tr, change to A, 1dc in each of next 2tr, 1ch, miss 1ch, 1dc in each of next 17tr] twice, placing last dc in 2nd ch of last st.

4th to 13th rows: Work 2nd and 3rd rows 5 times.

Cont in A.

14th row: 1dc in first dc, 2ch, 1tr in next dc, [1ch, miss 1dc or 1ch, 1tr in each of next 2dc] to end.

15th row: 1ch, 1dc in each of first 17tr or ch, [1ch, miss 1ch, 1dc in each of next 2tr, 1dc in next ch, 1dc in each of foll 2tr, 1ch, miss 1ch, 1dc in each of next 2tr, 1dc in next ch, 1dc in each of foll 2tr, 1ch, miss 1ch, 1dc in each of foll 17tr or ch] 4 times, placing last dc in 2nd ch of last st.

16th row: 1dc in first dc, 2ch, 1tr in each of next 16dc, [1ch, miss 1ch, 1tr in each of foll 5dc, 1ch, miss 1ch, 1tr in each of foll 5dc, 1ch, miss 1ch, 1tr in each of foll 17dc] 4 times.
Cont in B.

17th row: 1ch, 1dc in each of first 17tr, [1ch, miss 1ch, 1dc in each of foll 5tr, 1ch, miss 1ch, 1dc in each of next 5tr, 1ch, miss 1ch, 1dc in each of foll 17tr] 4 times placing last dc in 2nd ch of last st.

18th row: As 16th row.

19th row: 1ch, 1dc in each of first 2tr, [1ch, miss 1tr or 1ch, 1dc in each of next 2tr] to end placing last dc in 2nd ch of last st.

20th row: 1dc in first dc, 2ch, 1tr in each of next 16dc or 1ch sps, [1ch, miss 1ch, 1tr in each of foll 2dc, 1tr in next 1ch sp, 1tr in each of next 2dc, 1ch, miss 1ch, 1tr in each of foll 2dc, 1tr in next 1ch sp, 1tr in each of next 2dc, 1ch, miss 1ch, 1tr in each of foll 17dc or 1ch sps] 4 times.

21st row: As 17th row.
Change to A.

22nd row: As 16th row.

23rd row: As 17th row.

24th row: As 14th row.

25th row: Cont in A, 1ch, 1dc in each of first 17tr or ch, [1ch, miss 1ch, 1dc in each of foll 2tr, change to B, 1dc in next ch, 1dc in each of foll 2tr, 1ch, miss 1ch, 1dc in each of foll 2tr, 1dc in next ch, change to A, 1dc in each of next 2tr, 1ch, miss 1ch, 1dc in each of foll 17tr or ch, 1ch, miss 1ch, 1dc in each of next 2tr, change to C, 1dc in foll ch, 1dc in each of next 2tr, 1ch, miss 1ch, 1dc in each of foll 2tr, 1dc in next ch, change to A, 1dc in each of next 2tr, 1ch, miss 1ch, 1dc in each of next 17tr or ch] twice, placing last dc in 2nd ch of last st.

26th to 49th rows: As 2nd to 25th rows but using C in place of B on 17th to 21st rows.
2nd to 49th rows form tr and dc check patt.
Patt 60 more rows, so ending with a 13th patt row.

Last row: Cont in A, [ss in each dc or ch] to end.
Fasten off.

to make up

Press according to ball band. Using D, make 8 lengths of 200ch and 8 lengths of 160ch. Thread the longer chain lengths through the 1ch sps at each side of the vertical bands in B and C and the shorter chain lengths through the 1ch sps at each side of the horizontal bands in B and C. Using E, make 4 lengths of 200ch and 4 lengths of 160ch. Thread the longer chain lengths through the 1ch sps in the centre of each vertical band in B or C and the shorter chain lengths through the 1ch sps in the centre of each horizontal band in B or C. Darn in ends.

african beads
circular throw

This throw is inspired by tribal circular beadwork patterns. The beads are represented by simple grouped stitches in bright colours, with shades of natural and black for the background.

SIZE
94cm (37in) across

YOU WILL NEED
2 x 50g balls of Debbie Bliss Cashmerino Aran in each of natural (A), black (B) and camel (G)
1 x 50g ball same in each of burnt orange (C), magenta (D), cream (E) and blue (F)
5.00mm (US H/8) crochet hook

TENSION
The first 5 rounds measure 16cm (6¼in) across, 6 rounds in pattern measure 8cm (3⅛in), using 5.00mm (US H/8) hook. Change hook size, if necessary, to obtain this size centre and this tension.

ABBREVIATIONS
ch = chain; **cont** = continue; **dc** = double crochet; **foll** = following; **rep** = repeat; **RS** = right side; **sp(s)** = space(s); **ss** = slip stitch; **st(s)** = stitch(es); **tr** = treble; **2trtog** = leaving last loop of each tr on hook, work 2tr, yrh and pull through 3 loops on hook; **yrh** = yarn around hook; **WS** = wrong side; **[ ]** = work instructions in square brackets as directed.

NOTES
• When changing colours, pull through the last loop of the last stitch in the old colour with the new colour.
• When working the two-colour rounds you can either work over the yarn not in use or carry it across on the WS.
• When changing colours between rounds, you can avoid a lot of ends if you fasten off by enlarging the last loop, passing the ball through and pulling on the yarn to close the loop. Leave the yarn at the back of the work, catching it in if necessary, until that colour is used again.

throw
Using A, wind yarn around finger to form a ring.
1st round (RS): 1ch, 1dc in ring, 2ch, 15tr in ring, ss in 2nd ch. 16 sts.
2nd round: 1ch, 1dc in same place as ss, 3ch, [1tr in next tr, 1ch] 15 times, ss in 2nd ch. 32 sts.
3rd round: Using A, 1ch, 1dc in same place as ss, 2ch, [using B, 2trtog in 1ch sp, using A, 1tr in next tr] 15 times, using B, 2trtog in last 1ch sp, using A, ss in 2nd ch. 32 sts.
Cont in A.
4th round: Ss between first st and next 2trtog, 1ch, 1dc in same place as ss, 3ch, [1tr between same 2trtog and next tr, 1ch, 1tr between same tr and next 2trtog, 1ch] 15 times, 1tr between last 2trtog and first st, 1ch, ss in 2nd ch. 64 sts.
5th round: Using A, 1ch, 1dc in same place as ss, 2ch, [using C, 2trtog in next 1ch sp, using A, 1tr in next tr] 31 times, using C, 2trtog in last 1ch sp, using A, ss in 2nd ch.
Cont in A.
6th round: 1ch, 1dc in same place as ss, 3ch, [1tr in next tr in A, 1ch] 31 times, ss in 2nd ch.
Fasten off.
Join B in first 1ch sp.

7th round: 1ch, 1dc in same place as join, 2ch, [using D, 2trtog, using B, 1tr] in same place as join, [using B, 1tr, using D, 2trtog, using B, 1tr] in each 1ch sp, ss in 2nd ch. 96 sts.
Join A between first st and next 2trtog.
8th round: 1ch, 1dc in same place as join, 3ch, [1tr between same 2trtog and next tr, 1ch, 1tr between foll tr and next 2trtog, 1ch] 31 times, 1tr between last 2trtog and last tr, 1ch, ss in 2nd ch. 64 sps.
9th round: Using B, 1ch, 1dc in same place as ss, 2ch, [using C, 2trtog in next 1ch sp, using B, 1tr in next tr] 63 times, using C, 2trtog in last 1ch sp, using B, ss in 2nd ch. 128 sts.
Cont in B.
10th round: 1ch, 1dc in same place as ss, 3ch, [1tr in next tr in B, 1ch] to end, ss in 2nd ch.
11th round: Using B and E, work as 9th round.
12th round: Using B, work as 10th round.
Fasten off.
Join A in first 1ch sp.
13th round: Using A and D, work as 7th round. 192 sts.
14th round: Using A, ss between first st and next 2trtog, 1ch, 1dc in same place as ss, 3ch, [1tr between same 2trtog and next tr, 1ch, 1tr between foll tr and next 2trtog, 1ch] 63 times, 1tr between last 2trtog and last tr, 1ch, ss in 2nd ch. 128 sps.
15th round: Using A and F work as 9th round working instructions in square brackets 127 times. 256 sts.

16th round: Using A, work as 10th round. 128 sps.
17th round: Using A and E, work as 15th round.
18th round: Using A, work as 10th round.
19th round: Using B and C, work as 15th round.
20th round: Using B, work as 10th round.
21st round: Using B and D work as 15th round.
22nd round: Using B, work as 10th round.
23rd round: Using B and F, work as 15th round.
24th round: Using B, work as 10th round.
25th round: Using G and E, work as 15th round.
Cont in G.
26th round: 1ch, [1dc, 3ch, 1tr] in same place as ss, [1ch, 1tr in next tr in G] 3 times, * 1ch, [1tr, 1ch, 1tr] in next tr in G, [1ch, 1tr in next tr in G] 3 times, rep from * to end, 1ch, ss in 2nd ch. 160 sps.
27th round: Using G and C, work as 9th round working instructions in square brackets 159 times. 320 sts.
28th round: Using G, work as 10th round.
29th round: Using B and F, work as 27th round.

edging
Cont in B.
1st round: 1ch, [1dc, 4ch, 1dc] in same place as ss, * [2ch, 1dc in next tr in B] 9 times **, 2ch, [1dc, 4ch, 1dc] in next tr in B, rep from * 14 more times, then rep from * to **, 1tr in first dc.
2nd round: 1ch, 1dc in last tr, * [1ch, 1tr in next 4ch sp] 4 times, 1ch, miss 2ch sp, 1dc in next dc, [2ch, 1dc in next dc] 8 times, rep from * 15 times omitting last 2ch and dc, 1tr in first dc.
3rd round: Using B, 1ch, 1dc in last tr, * using E, 2trtog in next 1ch sp, [using B, 1tr in next tr in B, using E, 2trtog in next 1ch sp] 4 times, using B, miss 2ch sp, 1dc in next dc, [2ch, 1dc in foll dc] 6 times, rep from * 15 more times omitting last 2ch and dc, 1tr in first dc.
Cont in B.
4th round: 1ch, 1dc in last tr, * 1ch, [1tr, 1ch] twice in each of next 4tr in B, miss 2ch sp, 1dc in next dc, [2ch, 1dc in foll dc] 4 times, rep from * 15 more times omitting last 2ch and dc, 1tr in first dc.
5th round: Using B, 1ch, 1dc in last tr, * [using D, 2trtog in next 1ch sp, using B, 1tr in next tr] 8 times, using D, 2trtog in foll 1ch sp, miss 2ch, using B, 1dc in next dc, [2ch, 1dc in foll dc] twice, rep from * 15 more times omitting last dc, ss in first dc.
Cont in B.
6th round: 1ch, 1dc in same place as ss, * [3ch, 1dc in next tr in B] 8 times, [3ch, 1dc in next dc] 3 times, rep from * 15 more times omitting last dc, ss in first dc.
Fasten off.

to make up
Press according to ball band. Darn in ends.

scandinavian sampler *throw*

The fun, folksy effect for this patchwork throw is created by working Scandinavian-inspired motifs in cross stitch on a very simple crochet background that looks like a woven fabric.

SIZE
56 x 104cm (22 x 41in)

YOU WILL NEED
7 x 50g balls of Debbie Bliss Rialto DK in cream (A)
3 x 50g balls same in red (B)
4.00mm (US F/5) crochet hook

TENSION
11dc and 10 one ch sps measure 10cm (4in),
18 rows to 10cm (4in) over patt so each heart
block measures 10 x 10cm (4 x 4in) and each
flower block measures 27 x 17cm (10½ x 6¾in),
using 4.00mm (US F/5) hook. Change hook size,
if necessary, to obtain this tension and these
size blocks.

ABBREVIATIONS
ch = chain; **dc** = double crochet; **patt** = pattern;
rep = repeat; **RS** = right side; **sp(s)** = space(s);
ss = slip stitch; **st(s)** = stitch(es); **WS** = wrong
side; **[ ]** = work instructions in square brackets
as directed.

NOTES
• The crochet stitch pattern is given out for each
block and strip so you can be sure that you have
the correct number of 1ch sps to work the cross
stitch and the joins.
• To work the cross stitch motifs, use the arrows
marking the centre of the charts to place the
motifs on the centre of each block. If it helps,
mark out the area to be worked with contrast
tacking threads.
• Each marked square on the chart represents
one cross stitch. Each cross stitch is worked over
one double crochet. Use a blunt-pointed needle
and work the cross stitches neatly but not too
firmly, taking care to always take the thread
through the adjacent chain spaces each time. To
start and end the stitching, leave a long end and
darn it in behind the stitches afterwards. You can
work the cross stitches individually or in rows,
whichever you prefer but do make sure that the
top stitch of each cross lies in the same direction.
• Never carry the yarn across the back for more
than one stitch as it will show through, always
fasten off, count the stitches and spaces and join
yarn again in the new area.

heart blocks
Using A, make 22ch.
1st row (RS): Work into back strand of each ch, 1dc in 2nd ch
from hook, [1ch, miss 1ch, 1dc in next ch] 10 times.
2nd row: 1ch, 1dc in first dc, [1ch, miss 1ch, 1dc in next dc] 10 times.
2nd row forms patt.
Patt 15 more rows.
Fasten off.
Make 15 heart blocks.
Using B and Chart A, embroider a cross stitch heart motif on each
block.

flower blocks
Using A, make 58ch.
1st row (RS): Work into back strand of each ch, 1dc in 2nd ch
from hook, [1ch, miss 1ch, 1dc in next ch] 28 times.
2nd row: 1ch, 1dc in first dc, [1ch, miss 1ch, 1dc in next dc] 28
times.
2nd row forms the patt.
Patt 27 more rows.
Fasten off.
Make 4 flower blocks.
Using B and Chart B, embroider a cross stitch flower motif on
each block.

spacing strips

Using A, make 118ch.

1st row (RS): Work into back strand of each ch, 1dc in 2nd ch from hook, [1ch, miss 1ch, 1dc in next ch] 58 times.

2nd row: 1ch, 1dc in first dc, [1ch, miss 1ch, 1dc in next dc] 58 times.

2nd row forms patt.

Patt 3 more rows.

Fasten off.

Make 6 spacing strips.

join blocks

Join heart blocks

Place 5 heart blocks in a line. With RS facing, join B in 1ch sp at right of first row of first block on the left.

1st edging row (RS): 1ch, 1dc in same sp as join, [1ch, miss next row-end, 1dc in 1ch sp of foll row-end] 8 times.

Fasten off.

With RS facing, join B in first 1ch sp at top left of last row of 2nd block.

2nd edging row (RS): Work as first edging row but do not fasten off.

Hold blocks with WS together and first block facing you.

Joining row (RS): Ss in first 1ch sp of 2nd edging row, 1ch, 1dc same sp as ss, 1ch, 1dc in first 1ch sp of first block, [1ch, 1dc in next 1ch sp of 2nd block, 1ch, 1dc in next 1ch sp of first block] to end.

Fasten off.

Join 2nd and 3rd, 3rd and 4th and 4th and 5th blocks in the same way.

Join 2 more lines of 5 hearts blocks in the same way.

Join flower blocks

Make 2 lines each of 2 flower blocks, joining blocks at centre in same way as heart blocks.

to make up

Starting at the lower edge, lay out first spacing strip, first line of hearts, 2nd strip, first line of flowers, 3rd strip, 2nd line of hearts, 4th strip, 2nd line of flowers, 5th strip, 3rd line of hearts and 6th strip. Using B, and working [1dc, 1ch] twice into each join between blocks, work edging rows and joining row across between strips and lines of blocks in same way as joining heart blocks.

border

With RS facing, join B in 1ch sp at lower right corner.

1st round: 1ch, 1dc in same sp as join, * [1ch, miss next row-end, 1dc in 1ch sp of foll row-end or in dc in B over joins] to corner, 1ch, [1dc, 2ch, 1dc] in corner 1ch sp, [1ch, miss 1dc, 1dc in next 1ch sp] to next corner, 1ch, [1dc, 2ch, 1dc] in corner 1ch sp, rep from * once more omitting last dc in corner 1ch sp, ss in first dc.

2nd round: 1ch, 1dc in same dc as ss, * [1dc in next 1ch sp, 1dc in next dc] to corner, [1dc, 2ch, 1dc] in corner 2ch sp, rep from * 3 more times, ss in first dc.

Fasten off.

Press according to ball band. Darn in ends.

make a different size throw

You can vary the size of the throw by working more or less blocks and strips or you can change the design by working just heart blocks or flower blocks. All you need to make sure is that you have the same number of spaces both vertically and horizontally (counting each join between blocks as [1dc, 1ch] twice) so the strips and blocks will fit together. As a guide to estimating the yarn amounts for your variation on the design, each 50g ball of Rialto DK made 6 heart blocks and embroidering the 15 heart and 4 flower blocks took approximately 30g of Rialto DK.

chart A for heart block

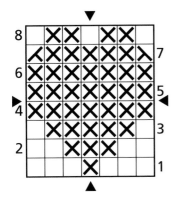

chart B for flower block

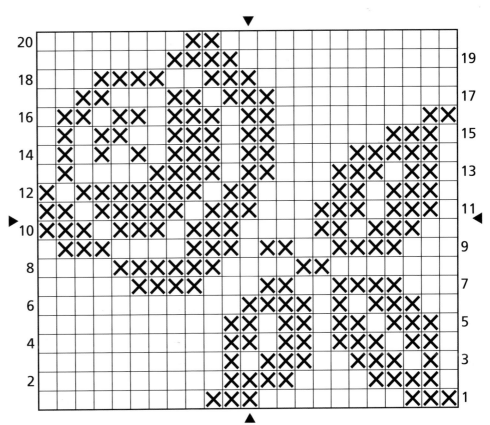

key

  = arrows mark the centre of the chart

☒ = cross stitch

⧅ = ¾ cross stitch

aran-style *throw*

Raised surface crochet stitches imitate the cable and bobble patterns associated with traditional Aran sweaters. To add to the authenticity, the throw is worked in creamy pure wool but would look just as good in a softer yarn or a pastel shade.

SIZE
74 x 96cm (29 x 37½in)

YOU WILL NEED
7 x 100g balls of pure wool Aran weight yarn
5.00mm (US H/8) crochet hook

TENSION
9 sts of panel A measure 6.5cm (2½in), 5 sts of panel B measure 4cm (1½in), 3 sts of panel C measure 1.5cm (⅝in), 47 sts of panel D measure 34cm (13½in), 12.5 rows to 10cm (4in) over all panel patt, using 5.00mm (US H/8) hook. Change hook size, if necessary, to obtain these tensions.

ABBREVIATIONS
ch = chain; **dc** = double crochet; **dtr** = double treble; **rep** = repeat; **RS** = right side; **st(s)** = stitch(es); **tr** = treble; **3trtog** = leaving last loop of each tr on hook work 3tr, yarn around hook and pull through 4 loops on hook; **trtr** = triple treble; **WS** = wrong side; **[ ]** = work instructions in square brackets as directed.

NOTES
• 100g in an Aran yarn can vary in yardage depending on the manufacturer. The yarn used for the throw had approximately 200 metres (220 yards) to a 100g ball. If the Aran yarn you choose is a different length, adjust the yarn amounts.
• When working the raised stitches around the stem of stitches two rows below, always take the hook to the front of the work.
• The raised stitches do not use the dc of the previous row; always miss 1dc for each raised stitch before continuing to work the row.
• The stitch patterns are given out as separate panels, which are placed on the first pattern row.
• To help keep your place when counting stitches for the panels, carry a thin contrast thread up between each of the panels.

panel A
Worked over 9 sts.
1st row (RS): Miss 2dc two rows below, 1dtr around the stem of each of next 2dc two rows below, 1dc in each of next 5dc, miss 1dc two rows below, 1dtr around the stem of each of next 2dc two rows below.
2nd and every WS row: 1dc in each st.
3rd row: 1tr around the stem of each of first 2dtr two rows below, 1dc in each of next 2dc, 3trtog in foll dc, 1dc in each of next 2dc, 1tr around the stem of each of last 2dtr two rows below.
5th row: 1dc in each of first 2dc, 1dtr around the stem of each of first 2tr two rows below, 1dc in next dc, 1dtr around the stem of each of last 2tr two rows below, 1dc in each of last 2dc.
7th row: 1dtr around the stem of each of first 2dtr two rows below, 1dc in each of next 5dc, 1dtr around the stem of each of last 2dtr two rows below.
8th row: As 2nd row.
Rep 3rd to 8th rows.

panel B
Worked over 5 sts.
1st row (RS): 1dc in each of first 2dc, 3trtog in next dc, 1dc in each of last 2dc.
2nd, 3rd and 4th rows: 1dc in each st.
Rep these 4 rows.

panel C
Worked over 3 sts.
1st row (RS): Miss 2dc two rows below, 1dtr around the stem of next

dc two rows below, 1dc in next dc, 1dtr around the stem of 2nd dc to the right of dc worked into two rows below.

2nd row: 1dc in each st.

3rd row: 1dtr around the stem of dtr on the left two rows below, 1dc in next dc, 1dtr around the stem of dtr on the right two rows below.

4th row: As 2nd row.

Rep 3rd and 4th rows.

panel D

Worked over 47 sts.

1st row (RS): 1dc in each of first 2dc, [* miss next 2dc two rows below, 1dtr around the stem of each of next 3dc two rows below, 1dc in each of next 5dc, miss 1dc two rows below, 1dtr around the stem of each of next 3dc two rows below, 1dc in each of next 2dc **, 3trtog in foll dc, 1dc in each of next 2dc] twice, rep from * to **.

2nd and every WS row: 1dc in each st.

3rd row: [* 1dtr around the stem of each of first 3dtr two rows below, 1dc in each of next 4dc, 3trtog in foll dc, 1dc in each of next 4dc, 1dtr around the stem of

each of last 3dtr two rows below **, 1dc in next dc] twice, rep from * to **.

5th row: 1tr around the stem of each of first 3dtr two rows below, 1dc in each of next 3dc, 3trtog in foll dc, 1dc in next dc, 3trtog in foll dc, 1dc in each of next 3dc, [miss next 3dtr two rows below, 1trtr around the stem of each of foll 3dtr two rows below, 1dc in next dc, 1trtr around the stem of each of 3dtr missed two rows below, 1dc in each of next 3dc, 3trtog in foll dc, 1dc in next dc, 3trtog in foll dc, 1dc in each of next 3dc] twice, 1tr around the stem of each of last 3dtr two rows below.

7th row: 1dc in each of first 2dc, 1dtr around the stem of each of first 3tr two rows below, 1dc in each of next 2dc, 3trtog in foll dc, 1dc in each of next 2dc, [1dtr around the stem of each of next 3trtr two rows below, 1dc in each of next 5dc, 1dtr around the stem of each of foll 3trtr two rows below, 1dc in each of next 2dc, 3trtog in foll dc, 1dc in each of next 2dc] twice, 1dtr around the stem of each of last 3tr, 1dc in each of last 2dc.

9th row: 1dc in each of first 4dc, 1dtr around the stem of each of next 3dtr two rows below, 1dc in next dc, 1dtr around the stem of each of foll 3dtr two rows below, [1dc in each of next 4dc, 3trtog in foll dc, 1dc in each of next 4dc, 1dtr around the stem of each of next 3dtr two rows below, 1dc in next dc, 1dtr around the stem of each of foll 3dtr two rows below] twice, 1dc in each of last 4dc.

11th row: 1dc in each of first 4dc, miss next 3dtr two rows below, 1trtr around the stem of each of foll 3dtr two rows below, 1dc in next dc, 1trtr around the stem of each of 3dtr missed two rows below, [1dc in each of next 3dc, 3trtog in foll dc, 1dc in next dc, 3trtog in foll dc, 1dc in each of next 3dc, miss next 3dtr two rows below, 1trtr around the stem of each of foll 3dtr two rows below, 1dc in next dc, 1trtr around the stem of each of 3dtr missed two rows below] twice, 1dc in each of last 4dc.

13th row: 1dc in each of first 2dc, 1dtr around the stem of each of next 3dtr two rows below, 1dc in each of next 5dc, 1dtr around the stem of each of foll 3dtr two rows below, [1dc in each of next 2dc, 3trtog in foll dc, 1dc in each of next 2dc, 1dtr around the stem of each of next 3dtr two rows below, 1dc in each of next 5dc, 1dtr around the stem of each of foll 3dtr two rows below] twice, 1dc in each of last 2dc.

14th row: As 2nd row.

Rep 3rd to 14th rows.

centre

Make 100ch loosely.

Set up row (RS): Work into the strand at the back of each ch, 1dc in 2nd ch from hook, 1dc in each of next 39ch, 3trtog in foll ch, 1dc in next ch, 3trtog in foll ch, 1dc in each of next 13ch, 3trtog in foll ch, 1dc in next ch, 3trtog in foll ch, 1dc in each of next 40ch. 99 sts.

Next row: 1ch, [1dc in each st] to end.

Work in patt.

1st row: 1ch, 1dc in first dc, 3trtog in foll dc, 1dc in each of next 2dc, work 9 sts of first row of panel A, 5 sts of first row of panel B, 3 sts of first row of panel C, 5 sts of first row of panel B, 47 sts of first row of panel D, 5 sts of first row of panel B, 3 sts of first row of panel C, 5 sts of first row of panel B and 9 sts of first row of panel A, 1dc in each of next 2dc, 3trtog in foll dc, 1dc in last dc.

2nd and every WS row: 1ch, [1dc in each st] to end.

3rd row: 1ch, 1dc in each of first 4dc, work 9 sts of 3rd row of panel A, 5 sts of 3rd row of panel B, 3 sts of 3rd row of panel C, 5 sts of 3rd row of panel B, 47 sts of 3rd row of panel D, 5 sts of 3rd row of panel B, 3 sts of 3rd row of panel C, 5 sts of 3rd row of panel B and 9 sts of 3rd row of panel A, 1dc in each of last 4dc.

These 3 rows set position of panels with 4 sts in patt at each side.

Cont in patt for 78 more rows, so ending with 3rd row of panels A and C, first row of panel B and 9th row of panel D.

Work 1 row dc.

83rd row: 1ch, 1dc in each of first 6dc, 1dtr around the stem of each of first 2tr two rows below, 1dc in next dc, 1dtr around the stem of each of next 2tr two rows below, 1dc in each of next 7dc, work 3 sts of 3rd row of panel C, 1dc in each of next 19dc, 3trtog in foll dc, 1dc in next dc, 3trtog in foll dc, 1dc in each of next 13dc, 3trtog in foll dc, 1dc in next dc, 3trtog in foll dc, 1dc in each of next 19dc, work 3 sts of 3rd row of panel C, 1dc in each of next 7dc, 1dtr around the stem of each of next 2tr two rows below, 1dc in next dc, 1dtr around the stem of each of foll 2tr two rows below, 1dc in each of last 6dc.

Fasten off.

borders

Make 13ch.

1st row (RS): Work in strand at back of each ch, 1dc in 2nd ch from hook, [1dc in each ch] to end. 12 sts.

2nd row: 3ch, miss first dc, 1tr around the stem of each of next 11dc, 12 sts.

3rd row: 1ch, 1dc in each of next 11tr, 1dc in 3rd ch. 2nd and 3rd rows form mock rib patt. Patt 80 more rows.

Last row: 1ch, miss first dc, 1dc around the stem of each of next 11dc, 1dc around end ch.

Fasten off.

Work 2nd border in the same way.

edging

Lower edging

With WS facing, join yarn around the stem of first dc of first row.

1st row: 1ch, [1dc around the stem of each dc] to end. 99 sts.

2nd row: 1ch, 1dc in each dc.

3rd row: As first row.

Fasten off.

Upper edging

With WS facing, join yarn around the stem of last dc in last row and work as given for lower edging.

Border edging

With RS facing, work 99dc evenly along one long edge of border.

Work 3 rows as given for lower edging.

Fasten off.

Edge 2nd border in same way.

Joining row

With WS of lower edge of centre to WS of border edging of first border, and border facing, join yarn in first dc of border edging, 1ch, 1dc in same place as join, 1ch, 1dc in first dc of centre edging, [1ch, miss next dc of border, 1dc in foll dc, 1ch, miss next dc of centre, 1dc in foll dc] to end.

Fasten off.

Join 2nd border to top edge of centre in same way.

Side edgings

With RS facing, work 2 rows of dc evenly along each side edge.

to make up

Darn in ends. Press according to ball band on WS.

kelim carpet *runner*

If you've ever wanted to own a hand-made carpet, here's your chance. Outlined eight-pointed stars in medallions are a characteristic motif found on the flat-weave carpets called kelims. Here they are interpreted in patchwork crochet using a simple stitch that looks like a woven surface.

SIZE
60 x 120cm (23½ x 47¼in) (excluding fringe)

YOU WILL NEED
Approximately:
100g of pure wool Aran in pink (A)
200g same in dark brown (B)
100g same in cream (C)
100g same in orange (D)
200g same in crimson (E)
5.00mm (US H/8) crochet hook

TENSION
Each patchwork star medallion measures 40 x 40cm (15¾ x 15¾in), from point to point, when pressed, using 5.00mm (US H/8) hook. Change hook size, if necessary, to obtain this size medallion.

ABBREVIATIONS
ch = chain; **cont** = continue; **dc** = double crochet; **foll** = following; **patt** = pattern; **rep** = repeat; **RS** = right side; **sp** = space; **ss** = slip stitch; **st(s)** = stitch(es); **tr** = treble; **2trtog** = leaving last loop of each tr on hook, work 2tr, yrh and pull through 3 loops on hook; **tog** = together; **WS** = wrong side; **yrh** = yarn around hook; **[ ]** = work instructions in square brackets as directed.

NOTES
• The star medallions are made up from simple shapes, edged and joined to make the motif.
• Medallions are joined and spaces at sides filled in to form the centre field. The borders are worked at each side of the centre field, then finished off with an edging and fringes.
• When changing colours, pull through the last loop of the last stitch in the old colour with the new colour. When working with two colours, either work over the colour not in use, or carry it across on the wrong side of the work.
• You can use more than one shade of any of the colours or invent your own colour scheme.
• When working edging rounds in B for the star medallion, instead of cutting and joining the yarn each time, fasten off by enlarging the last loop, passing the ball of yarn through and closing the loop leaving the B yarn at the back of the work ready for the next edging round.

star medallion
Centre square
Using A, make 8ch.
1st row (WS): Working into strand at back of each ch, 1dc in 2nd ch from hook, [1ch, miss 1ch, 1dc in next ch] 3 times.
2nd row: 1ch, 1dc in first dc, [1ch, miss 1ch, 1dc in next dc] 3 times.
2nd row forms the patt.
Patt 4 more rows.
Fasten off.
With RS facing, join B in 1ch sp at end of last row.
1st edging round: 1ch, [1dc, 2ch, 1dc] in dc at end of foll row, * [1ch, 1dc in dc at end of next row] 3 times, 1ch, [1dc, 2ch, 1dc] in dc at end of foll row, [1ch, 1dc in 1ch sp] 3 times, 1ch *, [1dc, 2ch, 1dc] in corner dc, rep from * to *, ss in first dc.
Fasten off.

corners
With RS facing, join C in a corner 2ch sp of centre edging.
1st row: 1ch, 1dc in corner 2ch sp, [1ch, 1dc in next 1ch sp] 4 times, 1ch, 1dc in corner 2ch sp, turn. 6dc.
2nd row: 1dc in first 1ch sp, [1ch, 1dc in next 1ch sp] 4 times, turn. 5dc.
3rd row: 1dc in first 1ch sp, [1ch, 1dc in next 1ch sp] 3 times, turn. 4dc.
4th row: 1dc in first 1ch sp, [1ch, 1dc in next 1ch sp] twice, turn. 3dc.
5th row: 1dc in first 1ch sp, 1ch, 1dc in next 1ch sp, turn. 2dc.
Fasten off.

Work a corner along each edge of centre in the same way. Join B in a 2ch sp of first edging round.

2nd edging round: 1ch, [1dc, 1ch, 1dc] in same 2ch sp, * miss first row in C, [1ch, 1dc in next row-end sp] 3 times, 1ch, [1dc, 2ch, 1dc] in 1ch sp of 5th row of corner, [1ch, 1dc in next row-end sp] 3 times, 1ch **, [1dc, 1ch, 1dc] in next 2ch sp in B, rep from * two more times, then rep from * to **, ss in first dc. Fasten off.

points

With RS facing, join A in a corner 2ch sp of 2nd edging round.

1st row (RS): 1ch, 1dc in same 2ch sp as join, [1ch, 1dc in next 1ch sp] 9 times, 1ch, 1dc in next 2ch sp, turn.

1st point

2nd row (WS): 1ch, 1dc in first dc, 1dc in next 1ch sp, [1ch, 1dc in foll 1ch sp] 4 times, turn.

3rd row: 1dc in first 1ch sp, [1ch, 1dc in next 1ch sp] 3 times, 1ch, miss 1dc, 1dc in last dc.

4th row: 1ch, 1dc in first dc, 1dc in next 1ch sp, [1ch, 1dc in foll 1ch sp] 3 times, turn.

5th row: 1dc in first 1ch sp, [1ch, 1dc in next 1ch sp] twice, 1ch, miss next dc, 1dc in last dc.

6th row: 1ch, 1dc in first dc, 1dc in next 1ch sp, [1ch, 1dc in foll 1ch sp] twice, turn.

7th row: 1dc in first 1ch sp, 1ch, 1dc in next 1ch sp, 1ch, miss next dc, 1dc in last dc.

8th row: 1ch, 1dc in first dc, 1dc in next 1ch sp, 1ch, 1dc in foll 1ch sp, turn.

9th row: 1dc in first 1ch sp, 1ch, 1dc in last dc.

10th row: 1ch, 1dc in first dc, 1dc in next 1ch sp. Fasten off.

2nd point

With WS facing, join A in next free 1ch sp of first row.

2nd row: 1ch, 1dc in same sp as join, [1ch, 1dc in next 1ch sp] 4 times, 1dc in last dc.

3rd row: 1ch, 1dc in first dc, [1ch, 1dc in next 1ch sp] 4 times, turn.

4th row: 1dc in first 1ch sp, [1ch, 1dc in next 1ch sp] 3 times, 1dc in last dc.

5th row: 1ch, 1dc in first dc, [1ch, 1dc in next 1ch sp] 3 times, turn.

6th row: 1dc in first 1ch sp, 1ch, 1dc in next 1ch sp twice, 1dc in last dc.

7th row: 1ch, 1dc in first dc, [1ch, 1dc in next 1ch sp]

twice, turn.

8th row: 1dc in first 1ch sp, 1ch, 1dc in next 1ch sp, 1dc in last dc.

9th row: 1ch, 1dc in first dc, 1ch, 1dc in 1ch sp, turn.

10th row: 1dc in 1ch sp, 1dc in last dc. Fasten off.

Work 2 points along each of the other 3 edges.

With RS facing, join B in a corner 2ch sp of 2nd edging round.

3rd edging round: 1ch, 1dc in same place as join, * [1ch, miss 1 row-end, 1dc in next dc] 5 times, 3ch, 1dc in next row-end sp, [1ch, 1dc in foll row-end sp] 7 times, miss 1 row-end, 1tr in 1ch sp of 2nd edging round, miss 1 row-end, 1dc in next row-end sp, [1ch, 1dc in foll row-end sp] 7 times, 3ch, [1dc in next row-end sp, 1ch, miss 1 row-end] 5 times, 1dc in 2ch sp of 2nd edging round, rep from * 3 more times omitting last dc, ss in first dc. Fasten off.

corner triangles

Using C, make 16ch.

1st row (RS): Work into back strand of each ch, 1dc in 2nd ch from hook, [1ch, miss 1ch, 1dc in next ch] 7 times.

2nd row: 1dc in first 1ch sp, [1ch, 1dc in next 1ch sp] 6 times.

3rd row: 1dc in first 1ch sp, [1ch, 1dc in next 1ch sp] 5 times.

4th row: 1dc in first 1ch sp, [1ch, 1dc in next 1ch sp] 4 times.

5th row: 1dc in first 1ch sp, [1ch, 1dc in next 1ch sp] 3 times.

6th row: 1dc in first 1ch sp, [1ch, 1dc in next 1ch sp] 2 times.

7th row: 1dc in first 1ch sp, 1ch, 1dc in next 1ch sp. Fasten off.

With RS facing, join B in first 1ch sp of first row.

Edging row: 1ch, 1dc in same place as join, [1ch, 1dc in next row-end sp] 5 times, 1ch, 1dc in 1ch sp of 7th row, [1ch, 1dc in next row-end sp] 6 times, do not fasten off.

join corner triangle

With RS together and triangle facing, hold corner triangle in a right angle corner between two points, cont in B.

Joining row: 1ch, 1dc in first 1ch sp of triangle edging row and 3ch sp of point edging row tog, [1ch, 1dc in next sp of each edging tog] 11 times. Fasten off. Make and join 3 more corner triangles.

side triangles

Using C, make 20 ch. Work in same way as corner triangles reducing the number of sts and sps by one on each row until there is one sp on the last row. Working eight 1ch sps along each side, edge row-ends of side triangles in the same way as corner triangles.

join side triangle

With RS together and triangle facing, hold side triangle in a wide angle space between two points, cont in B.

Joining row: 1ch, 1dc in first 1ch sp of triangle and 3ch sp of point tog, [1ch, 1dc in next 1ch sp of triangle and point tog] 7 times, 1ch, 1dc in dc of corner and tr between points tog, [1ch, 1dc in next 1ch sp of triangle and point tog] 7 times, 1dc in last 1ch sp of triangle and 3ch sp of point tog.

Fasten off.

Make and join 3 more side triangles. Do not fasten off after last joining row.

Cont in B.

4th edging round: Ss in 3ch sp at point, 2ch, 1tr in end 1ch sp of edging row of corner triangle, * [1ch, 1dc in

next 1ch sp of corner triangle] 7 times **, 1ch, placing first part tr in end 1ch sp of edging row of triangle and 2nd part tr in 3ch sp at next point work 2trtog, 2ch, placing first part tr in same 3ch sp and 2nd part tr in end 1ch sp of edging row of triangle work 2trtog **, [1ch, 1dc in next 1ch sp of side triangle] 9 times, rep from ** to **, then rep from * 3 more times omitting last 2trtog, ss in first tr.

5th edging round: Ss in last 2ch sp of 4th edging round, 1ch, 1dc in same place as ss, * [1ch, 1dc in next 1ch sp] 8 times, 1ch, [1dc, 2ch, 1dc] in 2ch sp, [1ch, 1dc in next 1ch sp] 10 times, 1ch, [1dc, 2ch, 1dc] in foll 2ch sp, rep from * 3 more times omitting last dc, ss in first dc.

6th edging round: Using B, ss in last 2ch sp of 5th edging round, 3ch, 1tr in same place as ss, * [using D, 2tr in next 1ch sp, using B, 2tr in foll 1ch sp] 4 times, using D, 2tr in last 1ch sp, using B, [2tr, 2ch, 2tr] in corner 2ch sp, [using D, 2tr in next 1ch sp, using B, 2tr in foll 1ch sp] 5 times, using D, 2tr in last 1ch sp, using B, [2tr, 2ch, 2tr] in corner 2ch sp, rep from * 3 more times omitting last 2tr, ss in 3rd ch.

Cont in B.

7th edging round: 1ch, 1dc in same place as ss, 1dc in first tr in B, [2ch, 1dc in each of next 2tr in B] to end, 2ch, ss in first dc.

8th edging round: Ss in last 2ch sp of 7th edging round, 1ch, 1dc in same place as ss, * [2ch, 2dc in next 2ch sp] to corner, [2ch, 2dc] twice in corner sp, rep from * to end omitting last dc, ss in first dc. Fasten off.

Make one more star medallion using the same colours and one using D for A and A for D.

join medallions

Join C in a corner 2ch sp at right of a side triangle of first medallion with star in A, with WS tog, hold corresponding edge of 2nd medallion with star in D behind.

Joining row: 1ch, 1dc in same place as join, 2ch, 1dc in corresponding sp of 2nd medallion, [2ch, 1dc in next sp of first medallion, 2ch, 1dc in corresponding sp of 2nd medallion] 8 times. Fasten off.

Join 2nd and 3rd medallions in the same way.

side triangles for centre field

Using E, make 34ch. Work in same way as corner triangles of medallion reducing the number of sts and sps by one on each row until there is one sp on last row.

edge and join centre field side triangle

With RS facing, join B in 1ch sp of first row-end.

Edging row: 1ch, 1dc in same place as join, [1ch, 1dc in 1ch sp of next row-end] 14 times, 1ch, [1dc, 2ch, 1dc] in 1ch sp of last row, [1ch, 1dc in 1ch sp of next row-end] 15 times.

Fasten off.

Join C in last 1ch sp of edging, with RS together hold triangle in front of edge to the right of two joined medallions.

Joining row: 1ch, 1dc in same sp as join and 2ch sp at corner of medallion tog, 1ch, 1dc in next 1ch sp of triangle and same 2ch sp at corner of medallion tog, [1ch, 1dc in next 1ch sp of triangle and next 2ch sp of medallion tog, 1ch, 1dc in foll 1ch sp of triangle and same 2ch sp of medallion tog] 6 times, 1ch, 1dc in next 1ch sp of triangle and corner 2ch sp of medallion tog, 1dc in 2ch sp of triangle and same 2ch sp of medallion tog, 1ch, 1dc in 2ch sp of join in C, 1ch, 1dc in 2ch sp of triangle and corner 2 ch sp of next medallion tog, 1ch, 1dc in next 1ch sp of triangle and same corner 2ch sp of medallion tog, [1ch, 1dc in next 1ch sp of triangle and next 2ch sp of medallion tog, 1ch, 1dc in foll 1ch sp of triangle and same 2ch sp of medallion tog] 7 times.

Fasten off.

Make, edge and join 3 more centre field side triangles.

edge sides of medallions

With RS facing, join C in dc in C of side triangle join at right of centre medallion.

Side edging row: 1ch, 1dc in corner 2ch sp of medallion, [1ch, 1dc] twice in each 2ch sp to next corner of medallion, 1ch, 1dc in corner sp, 1ch, ss in dc in C of join. Fasten off.

Using C, finish opposite edge of centre medallion, then work edging around remaining 5 sides of first and 3rd medallions in the same way, working [1ch, 1dc] twice in corner sps.

corner triangles for centre field

With WS facing, join B in corner 1ch sp on right of one slanted edge of first medallion.

1st row: 1ch, 1dc in same sp as join, [1ch, 1dc in next sp] 14 times.

Fasten off.

With RS facing, join E in first 1ch sp in B.

2nd row: 1ch, 1dc in same sp as join, [1ch, 1dc in next sp] 13 times, turn.

Cont in patt in same way as corners of centre square reducing the number of sts and sps by one on each row until there is one sp on last row.

Fasten off.

Work 3 more corner triangles in the same way.

edge field

With RS facing, join B in lower right corner 1ch sp.

1st round: 1ch, ** [1dc, 2ch, 1dc] in corner sp, up side edge work [1ch, 1dc in next row-end sp in E] 12 times, 1ch, 1dc in row-end sp in B, [1ch, 1dc in next 1ch sp of edging in C] 16 times, * 1ch, 1dc in row-end sp in B, [1ch, 1dc in next 1ch sp in E] 16 times, 1ch, 1dc in row-end sp in B, [1ch, 1dc in next 1ch sp of edging in C] 15 times *, rep from * to * across next side triangle and next medallion, 1ch, 1dc in corner sp in C, 1ch, 1dc in row-end sp in B, [1ch, 1dc in next row-end sp in E] 12 times, 1ch, [1dc, 2ch, 1dc] in corner sp, along top edge work [1ch, 1dc in next row-end sp] 12 times, 1ch, 1dc in next row-end sp in B, [1ch, 1dc in next 1ch sp in C] 17 times, 1ch, 1dc in next row-end sp in B, [1ch, 1dc in next row-end sp in E] 12 times, rep from ** down side edge and along lower edge, 1ch, ss in first dc. Do not fasten off.

1st side border

With RS facing, cont in B, ss in corner 2ch sp.

1st row (RS): 1ch, 1dc in same place as ss, [1ch, 1dc in next ch sp] to next corner. 111 sps.
Fasten off.

With RS facing, join E in first dc in B.

2nd row (RS): 1ch, 1dc in same place as join, 1dc in next 1ch sp, [1ch, 1dc in foll 1ch sp] to end, 1dc in last dc. 110 sps.

3rd row: 1ch, 1dc in first dc, [1ch, 1dc in next 1ch sp] to end, 1ch, 1dc in last dc. 111 sps.

4th row: Using E, 1dc in first dc, 2ch, 1tr in first 1ch sp, [using A, 2tr in next 1ch sp, using E, 1tr in foll 1ch sp] to end, using E, 1tr in last dc. Cont in E.

5th row: 1ch, 1dc in each of first 2tr, [2ch, 1dc in next tr in E] to end, 1dc in 2nd ch.

6th row: Using E, 1dc in first dc, 2ch, 1tr in foll dc, [using D, 2tr in 2ch sp, using E, 1tr in next dc] to end, using E, 1tr in last dc. Cont in E.

7th row: 1ch, 1dc in each of first 2tr, [2ch, 1dc in next tr in D] to end, 1dc in 2nd ch.

8th row: 1ch, 1dc in first dc, 1ch, [1dc, 1ch] twice in each 2ch sp, 1dc in last dc. 111 sps.

9th row: 1ch, 1dc in first dc, 1dc in first 1ch sp, [1ch, 1dc in next 1ch sp] to end, 1dc in last dc. Fasten off.

With RS facing, join B in corner st of field edging in B at start of border.

Edging row: 1ch, 1dc in first row-end in E, miss 2nd row-end, [1ch, 1dc] in 3rd, 4th, 5th and 6th row-ends in E, 1ch, [1dc, 2ch, 1dc] in corner row-end, [1ch, 1dc in next 1ch sp] to corner, [1dc, 2ch, 1dc] in corner row-end, [1ch, 1dc] in each of next 4 row-ends in E, miss next row-end, 1ch, 1dc in foll row end, ss in corner st of field edging in B.
Fasten off.

2nd side border

Work in same way as first side border, do not fasten off after working edging row, turn. Cont in B.

Edging round (WS): 1ch, 1dc in corner sp in B of field edging, * [1ch, 1dc in next 1ch sp] to corner, 1ch, [1dc, 2ch, 1dc] in corner 2ch sp, rep from * 3 more times, 1ch, [1dc in next 1ch sp, 1ch] to start of round, ss in first dc. Fasten off.

to make up

Using a damp cloth, press thoroughly on WS. Darn in ends. Using A, D and E make tassels by cutting four 15cm (6in) lengths of yarn for each tassel, folding yarn in half and looping through in alternate chain spaces along each short edge. Press and trim tassels.

make a bigger carpet

For a longer runner, make more medallions, join them in the same way and work longer borders to match. For a runner that's just a little bit wider, work more of the border pattern at each side. For a much bigger carpet throw, make more medallions and join them together at each side as well as above and below, making squares by working a 2nd triangle out from the chain edge of a centre field side triangle to fill the gaps between the medallions in the centre.

indigo ikat *throw*

The characteristic blurred patterning associated with the ikat weaving technique is interpreted here in a scrap yarn blue-and-white colour scheme inspired by antique Japanese work-wear. And there's a simple trick that makes the very effective two-colour crochet easy to do.

SIZE
71 x 120cm (28 x 47¼in)

YOU WILL NEED
Approximately:
150g pure wool or wool rich mix DK yarn, in shades of navy (A)
550g pure wool or wool rich mix DK yarn, in shades of pale blue, mid blue, bright blue and grey blue (B)
75g pure wool or wool rich mix DK yarn, in shades of cream and warm white (C)
4.00mm (US F/5) crochet hook

TENSION
For each half strip, the 42 sts measure 21cm (8¼in), the 53 rows measure 56cm (22in) both in chevron patt, centre square measures 12.5 x 12.5cm (5 x 5in), all using 4.00mm (US F/5) hook. Change hook size, if necessary, to obtain this size half strip and square.

ABBREVIATIONS
ch = chain; **dc** = double crochet; **foll** = following; **htr** = half treble; **patt** = pattern; **rep** = repeat; **RS** = right side; **sp** = space; **ss** = slip stitch; **st(s)** = stitch(es); **tr** = treble; **WS** = wrong side; **[ ]** = work instructions in square brackets as directed.

NOTES
• Each chevron panel is made up of three pieces, two chevron half strips are worked first then the square joins the strips at the centre.
• When changing colours, always pull through the last loop of the stitch before the colour change in the next colour.
• When working the chevron panel half strips, you can use scraps of yarn as short as 1½ metres (59in) for the dc rows or 3 metres (118in) for the tr rows.

chevron panel
1st half strip, 1st corner
Using A, make 2ch.
1st row: 1dc in 2nd ch from hook.
2nd row: (RS) 3ch, 2tr in dc. 3 sts.
3rd row: 1ch, 2dc in first tr, 1dc in next tr, 2dc in 3rd ch. 5 sts.
4th row: [1dc, 2ch, 1tr] in first dc, [1tr in each dc] to last dc, 2tr in last dc. 7 sts.
5th row: 1ch, 2dc in first tr, [1dc in each tr] to last st, 2dc in 3rd ch. 9 sts.
6th to 11th rows: Work 4th and 5th rows 3 more times. 21 sts. Fasten off.
2nd corner
Work as given for first corner but do not fasten off.
Join corners.
12th row (RS): [1dc, 2ch, 1tr] in first dc of 2nd corner, 1tr in each of next 19dc, miss last dc of 2nd corner and first dc of first corner, 1tr in each of next 19dc of first corner, 2tr in last dc. 42 sts.
13th row: 1ch, 2dc in first tr, 1dc in each of next 19tr, miss 2tr, 1dc in each of foll 19tr, 2dc in 2nd ch.
14th row: Using A, 1dc in first dc, 2ch, change to a shade of B, pulling through last loop of each tr with next colour, 1tr in first dc, * [1tr in A in next dc, 1tr in B in foll dc] 9 times, 1tr in A in next dc **, miss 2dc, rep from * to **, [1tr in B, 1tr in A] in last dc.
13th and 14th rows form the chevron patt. Note that the two-colour 14th row is used to change colours but it can also be worked in one colour.
Cont in B, patt 3 rows.
Changing shades of B or C on next and every foll 4th or 2nd row as wished, patt 36 more rows. Fasten off.

2nd half strip

Starting with A and changing shades as wished, work as first half strip.

square

Using a pale shade of B, wind yarn around finger to form a ring.

1st round (RS): 1ch, [1dc in ring, 3ch] 4 times, ss in first dc.

2nd round: Using first shade, ss in first 3ch sp, 1ch, [1dc, 5ch, 1tr] in first 3ch sp, change to 2nd shade of B, 1tr in same 3ch sp, * first shade, 1tr in next dc, [2nd shade 1tr, first shade 1tr, 3ch, 1tr, 2nd shade 1tr] in next 3ch sp, rep from * 2 more times, first shade 1tr in next dc, 2nd shade 1tr in first 3ch sp, ss in 2nd ch, ss in first 3ch sp, turn. Cont in 2nd shade of B.

3rd round (WS): 1ch, 1dc in same 3ch sp as ss, * 1dc in each of next 5tr, [1dc, 3ch, 1dc] in next 3ch sp, rep from * 2 more times, 1dc in each of last 5tr, 1dc in 3ch sp, 3ch, ss in first dc, turn. Change shades of B on every treble round in same way as 2nd round.

4th round: Ss in first 3ch sp, 1ch, [1dc, 5ch, 2tr] in same 3ch sp, * 1tr in each of next 7dc, [2tr, 3ch, 2tr] in next 3ch sp, rep from * 2 more times, 1tr in each of last 7dc, 1tr in first 3ch sp, ss in 2nd ch, ss in 3ch sp, turn.

5th round: 1ch, 1dc in same 3ch sp as ss, * 1dc in each of next 11tr, [1dc, 3ch, 1dc] in next 3ch sp, rep from * 2 more times, 1dc in each of last 11tr, 1dc in 3ch sp, 3ch, ss in first dc, turn.

6th round: Ss in first 3ch sp, 1ch, [1dc, 5ch, 2tr] in same 3ch sp, * 1tr in each of next 13dc, [2tr, 3ch, 2tr] in next 3ch sp, rep from * 2 more times, 1tr in each of last 13dc, 1tr in first 3ch sp, ss in 2nd ch, ss in 3ch sp, turn.

7th round: 1ch, 1dc in same 3ch sp as ss, * 1dc in each of next 17tr, [1dc, 3ch, 1dc] in next 3ch sp, rep from * 2 more times, 1dc in each of last 17tr, 1dc in 3ch sp, 3ch, ss in first dc. Fasten off.

join square to strips

Join A in a 3ch sp of square. With WS together hold a half strip behind the square.

Joining round: 1ch, 1dc in same 3ch sp as join, * 1ch, 1dc in 2nd dc of strip, 1ch, [miss next dc of square, 1dc in foll dc, 1ch, miss next dc of strip, 1dc in foll dc, 1ch] 9 times, 1dc in next 3ch sp of square, 1ch, miss centre 2dc of strip, 1dc in next dc, [1ch, miss 1dc of square, 1dc in foll dc, 1ch, miss next dc of strip, 1dc in foll dc] 9 times, 1ch **, [1dc, 1ch, 1dc] in next 3ch sp of square, hold 2nd half strip behind square, rep from * to ** to join 2nd strip, 1dc in first 3ch sp, 1ch, ss in first dc. Fasten off.

Make 2 more chevron panels in the same way, starting the half strips with a grey blue shade of B and the centre of the square

tip

To speed up working alternating colour trebles, why not try working two-handed crochet. Hold the yarn for one of the colours in the left hand. Hold the yarn for the other colour in the right hand along with the hook as if to knit. Work the stitches with the yarn in the left hand in the usual way. Work the stitches with the yarn in the right hand by wrapping the yarn over the hook (in the opposite direction to knitting) and pulling through as needed to form the stitches. Carry the yarn not in use loosely on the wrong side of the work. Of course, if you prefer, you can work the two colour crochet rows or rounds just by picking up and dropping the yarns as needed.

make a different size throw

For a shorter throw, simply work fewer rows in each of the half strips. For a longer throw, work more rows in each of the half strips. If you want to place the joining squares off centre, work more rows in one half strip and less rows in the other half strip. Always check that you have the same number of rows in adjacent half strips before joining with squares, so the squares line up when the panels are joined. For a wider throw, work one or more extra chevron panels. The edgings and border will always fit because they relate to the dc rows in the chevron pattern. Remember to adjust yarn amounts if changing the size of your throw.

with C for one panel and starting the half strips with a pale shade of B and the centre of the square with A for the other panel.

to make up

With RS facing, join A in dc at top left corner of a panel and work along long edge.

Side edging row: 1ch, [1dc, 1htr] in same dc as join, * [1ch, 1htr, 1dc, 1htr] between 2nd and 3rd sts of next dc row-end **, rep from * down first half strip, [1ch, 1htr, 1dc, 1htr] in 1ch sp at corner of square, rep from * to ** along 2nd half strip, omitting last htr. Fasten off.

Join A in dc at lower right of same panel and work along long edge in same way.

Edge the other 2 panels in the same way.

Join panels

Join a shade of B in first 1ch sp at lower edge of panel with A at each end and with WS together, hold panel with grey blue at each end behind it.

Joining row: 1ch, 1dc in same sp as join, 2ch, 1dc in first 1ch sp of panel at back, [2ch, 1dc in next 1ch sp of panel in front, 2ch, 1dc in next 1ch sp of panel at back] to end. Fasten off.

Join panel with pale blue at each end to panel with grey blue at each end in the same way.

Join ends of dc rows at centre of each strip.

Join A in dc in A worked in corner dc at top right of joined panels.

Upper edging row: 2ch, [1dc, 1htr] in corner dc, * [1ch, 1htr, 1dc, 1htr] between 2nd and 3rd sts of next dc row-end] 4 times, 1ch, [1htr, 1dc, 1htr] in joined dc row at centre of panel, [1ch, 1htr, 1dc, 1htr] between 2nd and 3rd sts of next dc row-end] 4 times, 1ch, [1htr, 1dc] in next corner dc, 1ch, ss in next dc **, 3ch, ss in dc at next corner, 1ch, [1dc, 1htr] in corner dc, rep from * along edge of next panel, then from * to ** along edge of foll panel ending with 2ch before the last ss. Fasten off.

Lower edging row: Join A in dc at lower left of joined panels and work as given for upper edging row.

border

Join a shade of B in a corner 2ch sp.

1st round: 1ch, [1dc, 2ch, 1dc, 1htr] in corner 2ch sp, * 1ch, [1htr, 1dc, 1htr] in next 1ch sp, rep from * to corner, 1ch, [1htr, 1dc, 2ch, 1dc, 1htr] in corner 2ch sp **, rep from * to ** two more times, then rep from * to corner, 1ch, 1htr in first 2ch sp, ss in first dc. Fasten off.

2nd round: Join A in corner 2ch sp and work as given for first round.

Darn in ends. Press lightly on WS.

how to *crochet*

getting started

I hope that you'll be so inspired by the designs in this book that you can't wait to get started. But before you begin, read through these notes and comments to help you get the best out of your chosen projects. If you're new to crochet or need to refresh your memory, there's a quick run through of all you need to know in the basic stitches section, plus a mini workshop on different ways of joining motifs.

choosing yarns

Where a specific brand of yarn is given in the instructions, it really is worth making the effort to track that yarn down as another yarn may change the character of the design. However, if you can't find the exact yarn, some of the following tips for working with scrap yarns will help you choose an alternative. Throughout the book, even where a specific yarn quality is given, I've named the colours as simply as possible rather than giving exact shade numbers, because colours are discontinued and new colours brought in as the seasons change. You may, of course, use whatever colours you like.

WORKING WITH SCRAP YARNS

Many of the projects in this book are scrap yarn projects. Some really do use up even tiny amounts of yarn, some are more odd ball projects, while others simply give you the freedom to buy just a few balls of yarn at a time, adding more as your afghan or blanket grows. There are lots of advantages to using scrap yarn; you cut the cost of being creative if you can raid your stash or swap yarns with friends rather than taking a trip to a shop and you can mix different brands of a similar weight of yarn to give a wider choice of colours.

Apart from the Seascape Wall Hanging, the scrap yarn projects use yarns of the same weight. But even yarns of the same weight may vary in thickness, so motifs worked in different brands of yarn may vary in size. Don't panic! Simply make sure that the different sizes are distributed evenly before making up the project, so the larger motifs will compensate for the smaller ones to give you average measurements overall.

CUSTOMISING THE PROJECTS

With scrap yarn projects, you can mix and match yarns to invent your own colour schemes and personalise your choice of design. For instance, you could follow the instructions for the Rainbow Baby Blanket but for a very different effect, use just

tones of naturals, creams, browns and greys. You could change the colours of the Kelim Runner to match a favourite rug, or instead of using the colours given for the Seascape Wall Hanging – which were inspired by a beach in Cornwall – you could create a sunset, a stormy sea or a tropical paradise. The key to substituting colours is to match the relative tones of the original then, even if your colour palette is lighter or darker, the design will still work. Imagine the Log Cabin Coverlet worked in soft pastel shades: as long as there is a difference in tone for each half square, the diagonal shadow design will still be apparent, but if you work colours at random although they may look pretty you will lose this aspect of the design.

If you're trying to decide on a colour scheme, spread out the balls of yarn you'd like to use, stand back and see what the overall effect is. Take out and put in different colours until you have roughly the amounts needed for your project. Sometimes a rather bland mix can be energised by a clashing colour, sometimes you can see what new colours you need to source – and sometimes you simply have to admit that although you'd like to use up that pea green from your stash, it isn't going to work here!

PRACTICAL CONSIDERATIONS

Although working with scrap yarns can unlock your creativity, there are some things to watch out for. At the start of each project I've tried to give an idea of the type of yarn used, the amount of yarn used to make the original, the fibre content and the colour range. If you use a different fibre mix, then it's possible that you will need a different amount of yarn. That's fine, just as long as you are aware of it. Below are some typical examples of how many metres/yards you might find, depending on the fibre content, in a 50g ball of DK weight yarn.

Cotton: 85 metres/93 yards
Pure wool: 116 metres/127 yards
Wool mix: 120 metres/131 yards
Acrylic mix: 150 metres/174 yards

All of the projects in this book are worked in natural fibre yarns or mixes with a high natural content. This is a very practical choice, especially when making a patchwork project, because it may be necessary to block or press the finished item thoroughly and natural fibres cope better with heat and damp.

Another thing to think about before mixing different fibre yarns in a project is how the yarns will behave when washed. If in doubt, always hand wash your handiwork using a liquid detergent and, if you wish, a softener. Most blankets or afghans can then be spun in the machine to remove excess water, though it's a good idea to protect the surface from rubbing by first putting the item in a pillowcase, or a duvet cover if it is very large. After spinning leave to dry, either laid flat or draped over a washing line if the weather is fine. Never tumble dry a hand-made blanket unless you are absolutely sure that it stated you can on the ball band of the yarn used. Be prepared to dry clean really delicate items.

does tension really matter?

You've sorted out the yarn and you're raring to go, will you really stop and work a tension swatch? Well, you might think that since it's not a garment, it doesn't have to fit – but think again. Each project has a tension or size of motif given. If you obtain this tension or size of motif, then your afghan or blanket will match the measurements and should take the amount

of yarn stated. If you do not get the same tension, then you may be disappointed with the fabric you make and you may need a different amount of yarn. If you want to experiment and you are happy with the result, that's fine. But if you don't check the tension first, then you are on your own!

basic stitches reference

All the projects in this book are made using just the simplest of stitches, mostly just chain, double crochet and treble crochet. Where a design needs more complex stitches or the stitches need to be grouped in some way, either decoratively or to shape the fabric, the exact way to work is given in the abbreviations in the instructions for that design.

Crochet stitches are worked into a base, which can be either a length of chain, or a ring made from chain or yarn. For most projects you'll need to start with a slip knot.

making a slip knot

1. Make a loop in the yarn, insert hook and catch the back strand of the yarn.

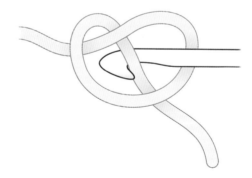

2. Pull loop through and gently tighten both ends of the yarn to close the loop on the hook.

holding the work

Hold the hook in your right hand, grip the slip knot between finger and thumb of your left hand and tension the yarn that goes to the ball of yarn over the other fingers and around the little finger. As you progress, move the finger and thumb of your left hand so that you are always gripping the work just below the stitch that you are working into.

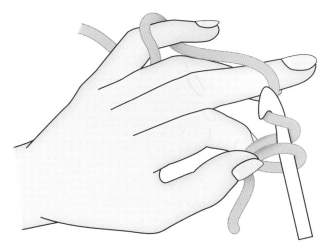

making a chain

1. Dip the tip of the hook to catch the yarn so it goes around the hook from back to front, this is the basic movement for making all crochet stitches. Draw the yarn through the loop on the hook to make a new chain loop. Do this for each chain required.

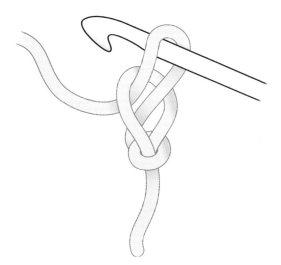

making a chain ring

1. Simply make the required length of chain, then insert the hook into the first chain, catch the yarn and pull it through the chain and the loop on the hook.

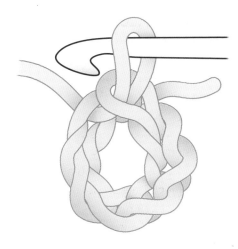

making a yarn ring

1. Make a loop in the yarn, insert hook and catch the back strand of the yarn just as in the first step for making a slip knot but do not tighten the loop on the hook. Catch the yarn and pull through in the same way as making a chain and tighten that loop on the hook, work the first round into the ring of yarn as directed, then pull the end to tighten the ring of yarn.

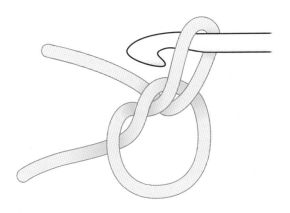

WORKING THE STITCHES

Crochet stitches are all made in a similar way to making a chain stitch, by catching the yarn and pulling it through. The amount of times the yarn is wrapped around the hook before catching and pulling loops through determines the height of the stitches.

slip stitch (ss)

1. This is the shortest stitch, it's like making a chain on the surface. Insert the hook into the designated stitch, catch the yarn and pull a loop through the stitch and the loop on the hook.

double crochet (dc)

1. There's a second step to this stitch. Insert the hook into the designated stitch and catch the yarn in the same way as making a slip stitch but pull the new loop through the stitch only, so making two loops on the hook. Catch the yarn around the hook and pull through the two loops on the hook. This stitch usually has a single chain worked at the start of a row or round to allow for the height of the stitches.

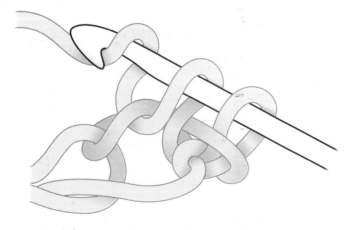

treble crochet (tr)

1. There are three steps to this stitch, making it taller. Make the number of chain as directed to bring you up to the height of the stitches and wrap the yarn around the hook once.

2. Insert the hook as directed, catch the yarn around the hook and pull a new loop through so there are three loops on the hook.

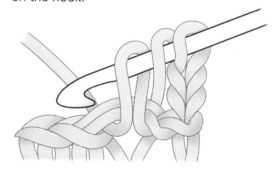

3. Catch the yarn around the hook and pull a loop through the first two loops on the hook.

4. Catch the yarn around the hook again and pull a loop through the remaining two loops, so you will end up with just one loop left on the hook. In fact when you finish any crochet stitch, you always end up with only one loop left on the hook.

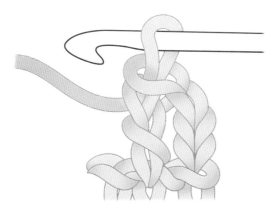

half treble (htr)

1. The height of this stitch is between a double crochet and a treble. Work the first two steps as given for a treble, then catch the yarn and pull a new loop through all three loops, so ending with one loop on the hook.

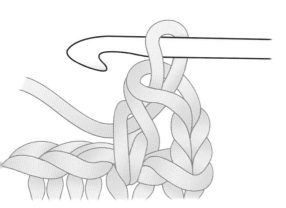

longer stitches

Longer stitches are worked in the same way as a treble but with extra wraps around the hook. So for a double treble (dtr) wrap the yarn twice, for a triple treble (trtr) wrap three times, for a quadruple treble (quadtr)

wrap four times, and so on. Each extra wrap around the hook will give one extra step when catching the yarn and pulling it through two loops at a time.

joining motifs

The finished effect of throws made using motifs or strips depends on the way in which the pieces are joined. The type of join to use to get the effect in the picture is given with each project but if you'd like to experiment, here are the three basic methods for you to try out. Always lay out the pieces in the colour arrangement you want before starting to join them.

sewing

The simplest way of joining is to sew the pieces together. For a decorative join that shows the chain edges of the motifs on the right side of the work, thread a blunt-pointed needle with the appropriate colour yarn and hold two motifs with RS together. Fasten on to the first stitch on the right with a couple of small stitches, then alternating between motifs, insert the needle through the top of each stitch just below the chain edge to over sew the motifs together.

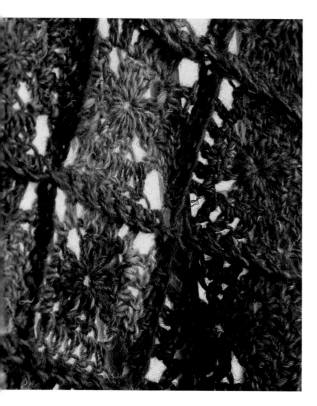

so on until all of the horizontal joins have been made. Keeping the same side facing, work the vertical joins in the same way.

zig zag join

Working a combination of double crochet and chain gives a more flexible fabric. This join is usually worked with the right side of the motifs facing which makes it easier to see where to place the stitches.

Using a crochet hook, join the yarn in corner stitch or space of the first motif and work 1dc, make 1ch, and work 1dc in the corresponding corner stitch or space of the second motif, make 1ch, work 1dc in the next stitch or space of the first motif, make 1ch, work 1dc in the next stitch or space of the second motif, continue working 1ch and 1dc, alternating between the two motifs until the edges are joined, then continue joining pairs of motifs until all the motifs in the line are joined. Join remaining lines of motifs in the same way.

You can vary this join by working more chain between the alternate dc stitches, by spacing the dc further apart along the edges of the motifs or by working into a decorative edging row.

double crochet join

This is one of the fastest, neatest ways to join motifs; it gives a firm, structured feel to the work. The double crochet stitches make a pronounced ridge on one side with unobtrusive stitches on the other side. If you want to make the join with the ridges on the right side, hold the motifs with the wrong sides together, if you want to make the join with the ridges on the wrong side, hold the motifs with the right sides together.

Using a crochet hook, join the yarn in a corner stitch or space, then inserting the hook, through the corresponding edge stitches or spaces of each motif work a double crochet stitch to hold the motifs together, continue working dc into each pair of stitches until all the stitches along the edges of the motifs have been joined. When two motifs have been joined work one or two chain stitches before joining the next pair of motifs. Continue in the same way until all the motifs in the first two lines of motifs have been joined, then taking care not to twist the first joining row, join the third line of motifs to the second, and

index

suppliers

IN THE UNITED KINGDOM

Debbie Bliss
Designer Yarns
tel: 01535 664222
www.designeryarns.uk.com

Sirdar and Sublime
Sirdar Spinning Ltd
tel: 01924 371501
www.sirdar.co.uk

Love Knitting
tel: 0845 544 2196
www.loveknitting.com

John Lewis
tel: 0345 604 9049
www.johnlewis.com

Deramores
www.deramores.com

IN THE UNITED STATES

Debbie Bliss, Sirdar and Sublime
Knitting Fever, Inc.
tel: 516 546 3600
www.knittingfever.com

Michaels
tel: 1-800-642-4235
www.michaels.com

Jo-Ann
tel: 1-888-739-4120
www.joann.com

Love Knitting
tel: 1-(866)-677-0057
www.loveknitting.com

IN CANADA

Debbie Bliss, Sirdar and Sublime
Diamond Yarn
tel: 416 736 6111
www.diamondyarn.com

Love Knitting
tel: 1 (877) 322-3799
www.loveknitting.com

IN AUSTRALIA AND NEW ZEALAND

Debbie Bliss and Noro
Prestige Yarns (PTY) Ltd.
tel: 02 4285 6669
www.prestigeyarns.com

acknowledgements

First of all, I owe a great deal to Cindy Richards for asking me to do this book and for giving me so much creative freedom. Thank you Cindy.

I'd also like to thank the team at CICO books, especially Pete Jorgensen whose calm involvement kept the plates spinning but never made me feel under too much pressure and Sally Powell, an inspiring art editor, for her sympathetic styling and beautiful vision.

Many thanks to everyone else who worked on this book: Marie Clayton, David Fordham, Michael Hill, Stephen Dew, Carolyn Barber and Beckie Maynes for the photography, and Catherine Woram and Sania Pell for the styling.

A huge thank you to Debbie Bliss and all at Designer Yarns and to Caroline Powell and all at Sirdar and Sublime for allowing me to use their beautiful yarns.

A vital part of a book like this is getting the instructions right. I cannot thank Susan Horan enough for her patient and thorough checking and for her involvement with the spirit of the designs.

For creative help when time got tight, many, many thanks to my friends: Lesley Stanfield for designing and making the Roses and Daisies Throw and the Puffs Baby Blanket, and Betty Speller for designing and making the Circular Coverlet, the Shetland-Style Shawl and the Seminole Blanket.

And a special thank you to my sister, Valerie Schofield, for her enthusiastic help with the cross-stitch embroidery for the Scandinavian Sampler Throw.